P9-DGS-625

Bee Cave Public Library
4000 Galleria Parkway
Bee Cave, Texas 78738

UMAMI BOMB

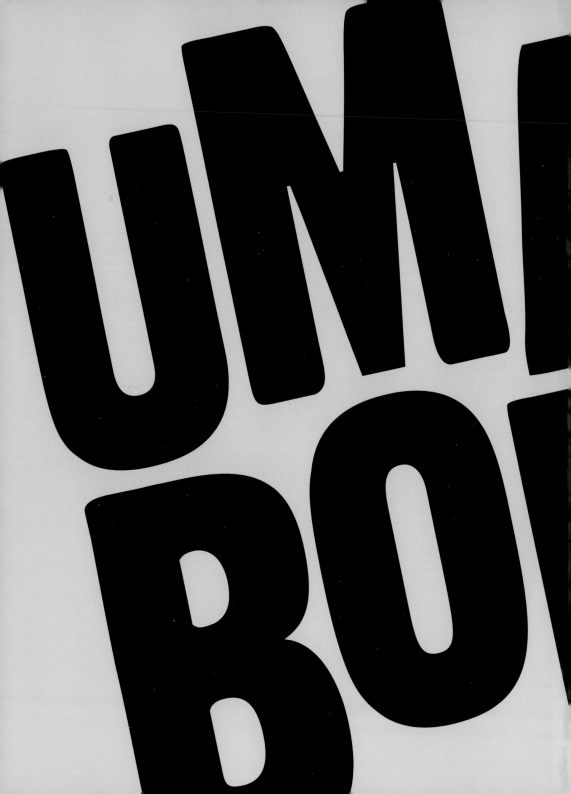

AMI MB

75
VEGETARIAN
RECIPES THAT
EXPLODE
WITH FLAVOR

RAQUEL PELZEL

WORKMAN PUBLISHING ✷ NEW YORK

Copyright © 2019 by Raquel Pelzel
Photography copyright © 2019 by Workman Publishing Co., Inc.

All rights reserved. No portion of this book may be reproduced—
mechanically, electronically, or by any other means, including
photocopying—without written permission of the publisher.
Published simultaneously in Canada by Thomas Allen & Son Limited.

Library of Congress Cataloging-in-Publication Data is available.

ISBN 978-1-5235-0036-9

Design by Rae Ann Spitzenberger
Photography by Kate Sears
Food styling by Kate Schmidt Buckens
Prop styling by Stephanie Hanes
Author photograph by Evan Sung
Additional credit: Splatter Icon: Milan M/Shutterstock.com cover and
pp. iii, ix, 5, 12, 15, 18, 21, 23, 26, 29, 32, 36, 39, 41-42, 48, 52, 55-56, 59,
61, 64, 68, 74, 77, 80-82, 85, 88, 90, 92, 94, 100, 102, 104, 108, 112, 114,
117, 120, 122, 124, 132, 135-136, 138, 141-142, 144, 147, 149, 152, 158,
160, 162, 165, 167, 171-172, 174, 180, 183, 186, 188, 190, 193, 196, 199,
202, 208, 211, 213, 215-216, 218, 221, 226, 229, 231.

Workman books are available at special discounts when purchased in
bulk for premiums and sales promotions as well as for fund-raising or
educational use. Special editions or book excerpts can also be created
to specification. For details, contact the Special Sales Director at the
address below or send an email to specialmarkets@workman.com.

Workman Publishing Co., Inc.
225 Varick Street
New York, NY 10014-4381
workman.com

WORKMAN is a registered trademark of Workman Publishing Co., Inc.

Printed in China
First printing July 2019

10 9 8 7 6 5 4 3 2 1

To Mom

You pronounce it
"ooooh-mommy."

5

CARAMELIZED ONIONS 128

6

MISO 154

UMAMI

\ ü-'mä-mē \

"A taste sensation that is meaty or savory and is produced by several amino acids and nucleotides (such as glutamate and aspartate)."
—Merriam-Webster Dictionary

"A strong taste that is not sweet, sour, salty, or bitter and that is often referred to as 'the fifth taste.'"
—Cambridge English Dictionary

"Good luck with Umami. I didn't understand a word in this* . . . but what I did get was interesting."
—Lauren Sayre (my mom)

*in reference to the article "Umami Taste Receptor Functions as an Amino Acid Sensor via Gα Subunit in N1E-115 Neuroblastoma Cells" by Yoshikage Muroi and Toshiaki Ishii (I do not know why she was reading the *Journal of Cellular Biochemistry*.)

INTRODUCTION:

A BOMB IS BORN

I'm always experimenting in my kitchen—with flavors, ideas, new recipes, odd obsessions (let me tell you about that time I tried to barbecue peanuts . . .). Because I don't eat very much beef, poultry, or pork (hardly any, really), I'm always interested in ways to make my vegetables taste extra, deeply, boldly, intensely, fantastically, rich-savory-comforting-eyes-roll-back-in-your-head awesome. I believe that if we could make our veggies taste extra great, everyone would eat more of them! And if we all ate more veggies, we'd improve the health of our bodies and our planet (I'm sure I don't need to tell you that raising livestock is an enormous contributor to carbon emissions, soil degradation, and drought).

So I started experimenting with all things umami. Umami is that special something that makes food taste better than good, more like amazing. Addictive. Can't-stop-eating-it incredible. It's why a simple dish of spaghetti marinara with grated Parmigiano-Reggiano cheese is so satisfying, why miso soup is so comforting, and why smoked salt makes everything *that* much better. Umami is known as the fifth taste (the first four are sweet, salty, bitter, and sour) and was discovered by a Japanese fellow named Kikunae Ikeda in 1908 when he got curious as to why dashi—that simple broth made from *kombu* (dried kelp seaweed) and *katsuobushi* (dried, fermented, and smoked fish, also known as bonito flakes) and sometimes little dried sardines, too—tasted so deeply delicious.

I quickly realized that I have always been obsessed with umami; I just didn't *know* it. It's why a sprinkle of Parm on just about anything heightens that dish's flavor; it's why grilled smoky mushrooms taste so good. Umami is a deeply satisfying taste, and lucky for us, umami is everywhere—it's in tomatoes and soy sauce, fresh and dried mushrooms, aged cheese, nutritional yeast (if you're not sure what this is, be prepared to have your mind blown), and miso, just to name a few (it's also in animal products like bacon and chicken broth—see page 4). If you eat a mostly plant-based diet, or even if you don't but you'd like to add more vegetables to your everyday routine, then you really need to pay attention to all the ways you can add umami to your beans, greens, and everything in between.

> **Umami is a deeply satisfying flavor, and lucky for us, umami is everywhere**

You can get super technical when talking about umami in terms of molecules and cellular composition, but here's a very simple explanation: Umami is what happens when proteins break down and amino acids and ribonucleotides are left to get crazy in your mouth. There are a few different kinds of aminos that contribute to umami, with glutamate being the most known (it's the "G" in MSG, aka monosodium glutamate, the manufactured form of umami) and common to cheese, miso, soy sauce, kombu, and tomatoes. When foods are fermented, preserved, aged, or even just browned or roasted, their proteins break down and the glutamate is activated, heightening the umami taste. For example, a fresh tomato has fewer glutamates than sun-dried or roasted tomatoes, and aged Parmigiano-Reggiano or aged Gouda cheese has way more than, say, fresh mozzarella.

BOMB SAUCE, page 208
(there's umami in that, too!)

UMAMI'S MEATY SIDE

Bacon. Chicken fat. Anchovies. Although umami comes in many plant-based forms, it is often associated with animal products. I believe that the secret to eating more meat-free meals is to make vegetables and dishes that don't rely on meat really sing. Adding caramelized onions and smoked salt to a veggie burger gives me just as much satisfaction as eating a grass-fed beef burger might—minus the environmental guilt. For me, eating clean and green is as much about sustainability and making an impact on our environment as it is about animal welfare.

If I'm cooking fish or shellfish, I do so only occasionally, and I always buy it from reliable, sustainably driven purveyors. I'm not a vegetarian or vegan. I eat a mostly pescatarian diet and include fish in my rotation about once a week; this is why I've included a few fish and shellfish recipes (see the bonus chapter beginning on page 224). You don't need to tattoo an eating plan across your forehead—and the way you eat can shift according to the seasons or how your body feels. I just encourage you to make healthy choices and think about the environmental impact of those choices.

It's long been known that raising livestock has far more negative implications on the environment than raising lentils and cabbage. Using umami to make my vegetables super interesting and intensely flavorful is how I never get bored of eating them, and how I use my wallet to cast a vote for environmental change and make a difference each and every day. Adding a little crispy-rendered bacon or using duck fat to roast potatoes will definitely offer umami, too. How often you want to incorporate these tactics into your cooking is up to you . . . but my hope is that by using this book, you find more flavor in vegetables and fewer reasons to lean on meat.

Disodium guanylate (or just guanylate) and disodium inosinate (or just inosinate) are the ribonucleotide components of amino acids— guanylate is found in mushrooms, and inosinate is found in animal proteins (beef, chicken, and fish). When used synergistically, for example glutamate + inosinate (think: soy sauce + sushi), the umami factor increases significantly. When several glutamate-rich ingredients are used together, the umami increases too, like tomatoes + cheese, or miso + nutritional yeast.

So how do you change your life and eat more vegetables and be satisfied and happy and at peace with the world? (I can help you with the first few bits, but you may have to dip into some other self-care genres to conquer that last part.) You cook more umami-rich food and marry umami ingredients together!

UMAMI BOMB: HOW TO USE THIS BOOK

Here's where this book comes in. Each chapter is devoted to an umami ingredient: aged cheese (Parmigiano-Reggiano and Gouda cheeses are two types that are the highest in umami, so I focus on them, though I also call for other aged cheeses like Cheddar and Pecorino Romano), soy sauce, tomatoes, mushrooms, caramelized onions, miso, smoke, and nutritional yeast. I'll explain what gives the ingredient its umami characteristic and then offer plenty of recipes to tap into that magic. There are loads of vegan options (marked with a **V**) and vegan-optional (**VO**) ones, too. Plus, you'll find an umami rating system based on the number of umami ingredients used in a recipe. Say I call for tomatoes, soy sauce, and aged cheese in a recipe—it will have 🌸🌸🌸 umami bombs.

CHAPTER

PARM & OTHER AGED CHEESES

NUTTY, BUTTERY, CARAMEL, SALTY, CRYSTALLINE

As cheese ages, its proteins break down and glutamates and free amino acids—the things that translate to delicious umami—are released. It turns out that Parmigiano-Reggiano cheese (aka "Parm") has more glutamates than even soy sauce (see Chapter 2). When you bite into a nugget of nicely aged Parm or Gouda and it crunches and its flavor explodes into a million facets of nutty, sweet, salty, funky, sharp deliciousness? That's actually umami you're tasting.

Both aged Parm and Gouda cheeses (not the buttery yellow Gouda you see in the supermarket deli aisle, but the butterscotch-orange wedge you see at cheese shops) have loads of umami and they enhance foods in so many ways. Add them to pasta for an easy salty-unctuous win. When you pan-fry grated Parm on its own, those clusters of free-roaming aminos (technically called tyrosine crystals) concentrate even more as they cook down and crisp in the skillet, becoming a crumbly, crunchy alternative to croutons. Aged Gouda is an unexpected sweet-savory addition to risotto, while sharp, aged Cheddar adds a salty, delicate, crispy-edged twist to morning waffles (with maple syrup, of course!).

BREAKFAST PASTA

SERVES 4

UMAMI BOMBS:

Kosher salt

1 pound dried spaghetti

3 tablespoons unsalted butter

¼ teaspoon crushed red pepper flakes

½ teaspoon freshly ground black pepper

⅓ cup panko bread crumbs

3 tablespoons extra-virgin olive oil

4 large eggs

¼ cup finely grated Pecorino Romano cheese

¼ cup finely grated Parmigiano-Reggiano cheese

1 tablespoon finely chopped fresh chives or parsley

On lazy weekend mornings (let's not be jokers, here— I'm not making this on weekday mornings!) when I'm too comfy to get out of bed to make breakfast and somehow the time seems to tick away into the late morning in the blink of an eye, I'll make this. It's carby and creamy and warm and delicious—like cacio e pepe with an egg or carbonara without the pancetta, depending how you choose to look at it. Pecorino Romano is a hard Italian grating cheese similar to Parm, but it's made from sheep's milk and has a sharper, more pungent taste.

1 Fill a large pot halfway with water and bring to a boil over high heat (less water makes for starchier pasta water and this will help your sauce cling to the pasta). Add 1 tablespoon of salt and the pasta and cook according to the package directions until the pasta is just shy of al dente (it should taste like it still needs 1 minute longer in the pot—it will be somewhat solid white at the core of a strand). Reserve 1 cup of the pasta water, then drain the pasta through a fine-mesh sieve. Return the reserved pasta water to the pot.

2 Meanwhile, melt 2 tablespoons of the butter in a large nonstick skillet over medium heat. Add

>>

the crushed red pepper flakes, black pepper, and bread crumbs, stirring everything into the butter. Add a pinch of salt and cook, stirring often, until the crumbs are golden brown, 3 to 5 minutes. Transfer to a plate and set aside.

3 Heat 1 tablespoon of the oil in the skillet for 30 seconds. Crack the eggs into the skillet and cook until the whites are solid but the yolks are still runny (you may have to cook them two at a time depending on the size of your pan).

4 While the eggs cook, finish the pasta: Place the pot with the reserved pasta water over high heat. Once the water starts to bubble, add the remaining 1 tablespoon butter and 2 tablespoons olive oil along with the drained pasta. Cook, stirring often to coat the pasta, for 45 seconds. Stir in the cheeses, chives, and 1 teaspoon of salt and divide among four bowls. Sprinkle with the bread crumb mixture, top each serving with an egg, and serve immediately.

PARM-BONE BROTH

SERVES 4

UMAMI BOMBS:

- 2 tablespoons canola or grapeseed oil
- 1 medium yellow onion, peeled and quartered
- 1 large shallot, peeled and quartered
- 2 ribs celery, roughly chopped
- 2 medium carrots, peeled and roughly chopped
- 1 broccoli stalk (with florets), roughly chopped, or 2 generous handfuls cauliflower florets
- 2 large garlic cloves, peeled
- 3 sprigs fresh parsley (flat-leaf or curly)
- 1 Parmigiano-Reggiano "bone" (rind)
- 2 teaspoons kosher salt, plus extra as needed
- 1 teaspoon whole black peppercorns

The heel of a wedge of Parmigiano-Reggiano is a magnificent source of flavor. When I'm grating Parm and come to the heel (aka the rind), I drop it into a ziplock bag and stash it in the freezer for up to a year (or let's be honest, two!). When I need a vegetarian broth, the "bones" are there waiting for me to turn them into this silky, rich, deeply nurturing broth—delicious on its own or used as the foundation for any soup you can dream up. (If you don't have the Parm heels on hand, you can buy a wedge, cut off the part good for grating, and just use the rind to make the broth.)

1 Heat the canola oil in a large soup pot over medium heat for 1 minute. Add the onion and shallot and cook, stirring often, until they are soft (you don't want them to brown; if they start to darken, reduce the heat to medium-low), 3 to 5 minutes.

2 Stir in the celery, carrots, and broccoli and cook until the celery begins to soften, about 8 minutes, then add the garlic. Pour in 12 cups of water and bring to a boil over high heat.

>>

3 Reduce the heat to medium and add the parsley, Parm bone, salt, and pepper. Set a cover on the pot so it is slightly askew to allow a little steam to escape and gently simmer until the carrots easily smash against the side of the pot, 30 to 40 minutes.

4 Turn off the heat, uncover the pot, and set aside until the broth is just warm (or completely cooled to room temperature), 1 to 2 hours. Strain the broth through a fine-mesh sieve and into an airtight container. Taste and add more salt if needed.

Use immediately or cover and refrigerate for up to 5 days. Return to a boil for 30 seconds before using.

STOCK TIP

When chopping, trimming, and peeling vegetables, save the odds and ends in a ziplock bag in the freezer. Add these scraps to your Parm-Bone Broth, or use them to make a mini batch of vegetable stock whenever you need just a couple of cups or want to make a small portion of soup.

PARM-BONE MINESTRONE

SERVES 4 TO 6

UMAMI BOMBS: ● ● ●

¼ cup extra-virgin olive oil

1 large yellow onion, peeled and finely chopped

2 medium carrots, peeled and finely chopped

2 ribs celery, finely chopped

1 large red bell pepper, halved, seeded, and finely chopped

2 teaspoons kosher salt, plus extra as needed

1 teaspoon freshly ground black pepper

6 medium garlic cloves, peeled and finely chopped

¼ cup finely chopped fresh herbs (such as parsley, rosemary, sage, and/or thyme—alone or in any combination)

2 teaspoons smoked paprika

2 tablespoons double-concentrated tomato paste (or ¼ cup regular tomato paste; see Note)

One of my favorite things to serve for dinner when friends come over is (brace yourself) soup! I love having it simmering when guests arrive—even the idea of soup is so welcoming, like a bear hug. I especially love the old-school comfy vibes that minestrone offers. All you need on the side is a salad and some garlic bread or grilled cheese sandwiches (page 149) and you're golden. I like when the pasta in the soup gets a little soft, but if that's not your jam, you can cook the pasta separately in boiling water, drain it, and add some to each bowl of soup before serving (if you plan on refrigerating leftovers, cooking the pasta separately is the way to go).

1 Heat the oil in a large soup pot over medium-high heat. Add the onion, carrots, celery, red bell pepper, salt, and black pepper and reduce the heat to medium-low. Cook, stirring occasionally, until the onion is tender, about 5 minutes.

2 Stir in the garlic, herbs, and smoked paprika. Once the garlic becomes fragrant, 30 seconds to 1 minute, stir in the tomato paste. Cook until the paste darkens, 2 to 3 minutes, then add the canned tomatoes. Pour in the Parm-Bone Broth and stir, scraping any browned bits up from the bottom of the pot.

1 can (28 ounces) chopped tomatoes (preferably fire-roasted), with juices

10 cups Parm-Bone Broth (page 15) or vegetable broth

1 head escarole, core removed and leaves roughly chopped

1 can (15 ounces) cannellini beans, drained and rinsed

1 cup dried small pasta (like orzo, elbows, or ditalini)

¼ cup fresh basil leaves, stacked, rolled, and sliced crosswise into thin ribbons, for garnish

Freshly grated Parmigiano-Reggiano cheese, for garnish (optional)

3 Bring the broth to a boil over high heat. Add the escarole, beans, and pasta and cook according to the directions on the pasta package, until the pasta is al dente. Add more salt to taste and add water to thin the soup if needed. Serve hot, sprinkled with fresh basil and Parmigiano-Reggiano cheese.

The soup will keep, in an airtight container in the refrigerator, for up to 5 days.

NOTE: *Double-concentrated tomato paste is available in most grocery stores—usually in easy-squeeze tubes. I find it less wasteful than opening a can.*

SHATTERED FRICO CRISPS AND GREEN SALAD

SERVES 4

UMAMI BOMBS: ◉

FOR THE FRICO CRISPS

¾ cup coarsely grated Parmigiano-Reggiano cheese

1 tablespoon all-purpose flour

¼ teaspoon garlic powder

FOR THE SALAD

½ small shallot, peeled and very finely chopped

3 tablespoons fresh lemon juice

½ teaspoon kosher salt, plus extra as needed

1 large garlic clove, peeled and halved

1 teaspoon Dijon mustard

Freshly ground black pepper

⅓ cup extra-virgin olive oil

8 cups greens (such as kale ribbons, baby spinach, arugula, and/or chopped romaine)

½ cup roughly chopped tender fresh herbs (such as basil, tarragon, chervil, parsley, and/or chives)

When Parmigiano-Reggiano is baked or fried, it melts into a thin and shatteringly crisp disk—called a frico—that adds a wonderfully crunchy, nutty, savory texture to salad and is a great (gluten-free!) replacement for croutons or bread crumbs. Here I dress a simple combination of greens and herbs with a Dijon vinaigrette so the pungency of the frico easily shines. You can make the crisps a couple of hours ahead of time (just keep them uncovered on the sheet pan) and sprinkle them over the salad just before serving.

1 *Make the frico crisps:* Preheat the oven to 375°F. Line a rimmed sheet pan with parchment paper or a nonstick baking mat.

2 Stir together the cheese, flour, and garlic powder in a medium bowl. Turn the mixture out onto the center of the prepared pan and spread into a uniformly thick 8-inch circle. Bake until evenly browned, about 10 minutes. Remove from the oven, set aside to cool, and break into small pieces.

3 *Make the salad:* Combine the shallot, lemon juice, and salt in a small bowl and set aside.

4 Rub the inside of a large salad bowl (preferably a wooden one) with the cut side of the garlic clove. Pour the shallot mixture into the bowl and whisk in the mustard and pepper to taste, then slowly whisk in the oil until you have a creamy emulsion. Add the greens and herbs and toss gently to combine. Taste a leaf for salt and add more if needed (but remember that the crisps will add a salty taste). Sprinkle the frico crisps over the salad and serve immediately.

1 pound green beans,
ends snapped

2½ teaspoons
kosher salt

Juice of ½ lemon

1 tablespoon
champagne or
rice vinegar

½ teaspoon honey

5 tablespoons extra-
virgin olive oil

1 head radicchio, cored
and halved lengthwise

½ cup fresh mint
leaves, stacked,
rolled, and thinly
sliced crosswise

1½ cups (4 to 5 ounces)
finely grated
Parmigiano-Reggiano
cheese (preferably
grated using a rasp-
style grater so it is
nice and fluffy)

Freshly ground black
pepper

GREEN BEAN AND CHARRED RADICCHIO SALAD

WITH LOTS OF PARM

Have you ever charred lettuce? If you haven't, be ready to have your mind blown—seriously, this is a game changer. Not only does heat add a beautifully nuanced and smoky flavor, but the outside leaves get nice and charred while the inside leaves stay cool, fresh, and crisp. I use my broiler to get the job done, but you can use your grill, too, for an extra smoky taste (and your salad will be even better for it). The finely grated Parmigiano-Reggiano cheese covers this salad like snow and really makes it so good. For another grilled salad, check out the Caesar riff on page 180.

1 Bring a large saucepan of water to a boil over high heat. Add the green beans and 2 teaspoons of the salt. Boil the beans until they are tender, about 8 minutes. Drain the beans in a colander and run them under cold water to stop the cooking process. Set the green beans aside.

2 Whisk the lemon juice, vinegar, and honey together in a large bowl, and then slowly whisk in 4 tablespoons of the oil until the vinaigrette is creamy. Add the green beans and toss to combine.

3 Adjust an oven rack to the upper-middle position and heat the broiler to high. Place the radicchio on a rimmed sheet pan and drizzle with the remaining 1 tablespoon of oil, then season with the remaining ½ teaspoon of salt. Broil the radicchio until the exposed leaves become dark and crisp, about 5 minutes (watch the radicchio closely, as broiler intensities vary).

4 Transfer the radicchio to a cutting board, let cool slightly, and then thinly slice into ribbons. Add it to the green beans and toss to combine. Transfer to a platter and sprinkle with the mint leaves, cheese, and a few cracks of black pepper. Serve immediately.

1¼ cups all-purpose
flour

½ teaspoon sugar

½ teaspoon kosher salt

¼ cup whole milk

2 tablespoons unsalted
butter, cut into
4 pieces

4 large eggs

1 ounce Gruyère
cheese, grated on the
medium-hole side of
a box grater (⅓ cup)

1 ounce Gouda cheese,
grated on the
medium-hole side of
a box grater (⅓ cup)

1 ounce Pecorino
Romano cheese,
grated on the
medium-hole side of
a box grater (⅓ cup)

½ teaspoon freshly
ground black pepper

THREE-CHEESE GOUGÈRES

If you're having a party or are asked to bring something to a party, this is the one. Gougères are little two- or three-bite cheese puffs, based on pâte à choux, an egg and flour paste that is, incidentally, also the base for cream puffs, éclairs, and even beignets (when fried). Usually recipes call for adding Gruyère to the choux base, but I'm adding aged Gouda and Pecorino Romano as well, just for kicks.

1 Adjust an oven rack to the upper-middle position and preheat the oven to 425°F. Line a rimmed sheet pan with parchment paper or a nonstick baking mat.

2 Combine the flour, sugar, and salt in a medium bowl and set aside.

3 Place the milk, ⅔ cup of water, and the butter in a medium saucepan and bring to a simmer over medium-high heat, swirling occasionally to melt the butter, 1 to 2 minutes.

4 Add the flour mixture to the milk mixture and use a wooden spoon to stir to combine. Keep stirring until the ingredients come together to make

a smooth dough ball that cleans the side of the pan. Transfer the dough to the bowl of a stand mixer (or a large bowl if using a hand mixer) fitted with the paddle attachment.

5 Turn the mixer on to medium-low speed and beat the dough for 10 seconds to allow some heat to escape, then start to add the eggs, one at a time, mixing well to incorporate before adding the next egg. With the last egg, add the grated cheeses and black pepper and beat until the dough is smooth and shiny, 2½ to 3 minutes.

6 Use a large spoon to drop dollops the size of ping-pong balls onto the sheet pan, leaving about 1 inch between mounds. Dip the spoon in water and use the rounded side to press down on the center of each mound slightly, just to eliminate any peaks and smooth out the shape.

7 Bake the gougères until they puff and brown slightly, 12 to 15 minutes. Reduce the oven temperature to 350°F and continue to bake until the puffs are golden on all sides, 20 to 25 minutes longer. Remove from the oven and let cool a few minutes before serving.

The gougères are ideally served warm and within 30 minutes of baking, but you can make them a few hours ahead; store them at room temperature and warm them in a 300°F oven before serving.

2 tablespoons extra-virgin olive oil

1 large yellow onion, peeled and finely chopped

1 teaspoon kosher salt, plus extra as needed

½ teaspoon freshly ground black pepper

3 large garlic cloves, peeled and finely chopped

2 teaspoons finely chopped fresh rosemary

1½ cups Arborio rice, rinsed under cold water and drained

1 cup dry white wine

4 cups hot Parm-Bone Broth (page 15) or vegetable broth

½ pound asparagus, ends trimmed and stems and spears thinly sliced crosswise

1 cup freshly shelled or frozen peas

3 ounces aged Gouda cheese, rind removed, plus extra for serving

2 tablespoons unsalted butter

1 tablespoon finely chopped fresh chives

SPRINGTIME RISOTTO
WITH AGED GOUDA, ASPARAGUS, AND PEAS

The season influences what goes into my risotto more than my mood. In the fall it's wild mushrooms, and in the winter it's squash and thyme. In the spring, when I am craving green-green-green, it's asparagus, peas, and chives. The caramely flavor of aged Gouda brings out the sweetness in the asparagus, but of course Parmigiano-Reggiano or Pecorino Romano is tasty, too.

1 Heat the oil in a large heavy-bottomed pot over medium-high heat. Add the onion, salt, and pepper and cook, stirring occasionally, until the edges of the onion darken, about 3 minutes. Stir in the garlic and rosemary and cook, stirring often, until the garlic smells fragrant, 30 seconds to 1 minute.

2 Stir in the rice and cook, stirring often, until the rice begins to turn opaque and smell toasty, 2 to 3 minutes. Add the wine, reduce the heat to medium-low, and cook, stirring often, until the wine is nearly absorbed (when you drag a wooden spoon through the middle of the rice, the pan will still look wet but most of the liquid will have been absorbed), 2 to 4 minutes.

»

3 Stir in ¾ cup of the broth. Cook, stirring every minute or two, until most of the broth is absorbed (you don't want the pan to be bone-dry—the mixture should look juicy, not soupy)—this will take 3 to 4 minutes. Continue to add the broth ¾ cup at a time, until you have about 1 cup of liquid left, 16 minutes or so—the rice should be just shy of al dente (it will still be a little white and undercooked at the core). Add ¾ cup of the broth with the asparagus (now you'll have ¼ cup of broth left). Cook, stirring, until the rice is al dente and creamy, 3 to 4 minutes longer. Stir in the peas, cheese, butter, and remaining broth and turn off the heat. Let the risotto stand for 1 minute, stirring once or twice, to allow the peas to warm through and the cheese to melt in.

4 Stir in the chives and add salt to taste. Divide the risotto among four bowls and serve immediately, with extra cheese grated on top if you like.

FALL MUSHROOM RISOTTO: Substitute Parmigiano-Reggiano for the Gouda and 1½ pounds of stemmed and sliced wild mushrooms (such as shiitakes, maitakes, creminis, or chanterelles) for the asparagus and peas. Sauté the mushrooms in 2 tablespoons of butter and 2 tablespoons of olive oil with ½ teaspoon of salt. Once the mushrooms release their liquid and brown completely, becoming somewhat crispy around the edges, stir half into the risotto. Reserve the rest to sprinkle over the risotto along with more grated cheese before serving.

WINTER SQUASH AND THYME RISOTTO: Substitute 1½ ounces of Pecorino Romano for half of the Gouda; 1 pound of ½-inch squash cubes (kabocha squash is my favorite, but butternut or acorn is good, too) for the asparagus and peas; and finely chopped fresh thyme for the rosemary. Preheat the oven to 400°F and toss the squash with 2 tablespoons of canola oil and the thyme. Roast in the oven, stirring occasionally, until the squash is tender and browned in spots, 15 to 20 minutes. Remove from the oven and stir into the risotto with the cheese. Serve with more grated cheese alongside.

FOR THE DOUGH

4 cups all-purpose flour

2 tablespoons sugar

2 teaspoons baking powder

2 teaspoons freshly ground black pepper

1 tablespoon fresh thyme leaves

1 teaspoon kosher salt

1½ cups (3 sticks) cold unsalted butter, cut into small pieces

4 ounces smoked Gouda cheese, grated on the medium-hole side of a box grater (about 1⅓ cups)

2 large egg yolks

⅔ cup ice water, plus extra as needed

GOUDA-APPLE-THYME GALETTES

I have a secret ingredient that I add to pie dough to give it a little extra tenderness and cushion: baking powder. I'm pretty sure I learned this trick from Ina Garten, who adds it to her pastry topping for a lobster pot pie—once I tried it, that was that. There's a double hit of Gouda—smoked in the pie pastry and aged that gets grated over the apples. I love this with pears, too, and yes, you can absolutely do this for breakfast or brunch.

1 *Make the dough:* Place the flour, sugar, baking powder, pepper, thyme, and salt in the bowl of a food processor and process for 10 seconds to combine (if making the dough by hand, whisk the dry ingredients together in a large bowl). Add the butter and smoked Gouda and pulse until there aren't any pieces larger than a small pea, about eight 1-second pulses (or use your fingers to work the butter into the flour mixture until the butter pieces are no larger than a small pea, and then add the cheese). Add the egg yolks, one at a time, pulsing the mixture between additions. Then, while pulsing, start to drizzle in the water. (If making the dough by hand, use a fork to incorporate the egg yolks and water.) Once all the ice water is added, take a small bit of the dough and

FOR THE GALETTES

4 Granny Smith apples, peeled, halved, cored, and sliced ¼ inch thick

4 tablespoons (½ stick) unsalted butter, melted

3 tablespoons maple syrup

Zest and juice of ½ lemon

Kosher salt

Aged Gouda cheese, for grating

1 large egg

Vanilla ice cream, for serving (optional)

squeeze it in your palm. If it comes together readily and doesn't look dry or crumble apart easily, it is done; if the dough crumbles apart, add another 2 to 3 tablespoons of ice water.

2 Transfer the dough to a cutting board and press and pat it into a ¾-inch-thick disk. Divide the dough into six equal pieces (like a pie) and then press each into a ½-inch-thick disk (don't knead the dough—just use your palms to press it into round disks). Wrap each piece in plastic wrap and refrigerate for at least 20 minutes or up to 2 days.

3 *Assemble the galettes:* Place the apples in a large bowl. Add the melted butter, maple syrup, lemon zest and juice, and a pinch of salt and toss to combine. Set aside.

4 Line two rimmed sheet pans with parchment paper or nonstick baking mats. Remove the dough from the refrigerator and let it sit out to soften, 15 minutes. Roll each disk between pieces of plastic wrap or parchment paper into a 9- to 10-inch circle that's about ¼ inch thick. Lift the top piece of plastic off each round of dough and divide the apples among them, leaving a 3-inch border at the edges. Fold the edges of the dough over the apple slices, loosely pleating the dough and leaving the center exposed. Use a metal spatula to transfer the galettes to the prepared sheet pans, placing three galettes on each sheet pan. Chill the galettes for

1 hour. (The galettes can be refrigerated for up to 4 hours before baking. I have refrigerated them overnight, and while they were still tasty, they were not quite as well structured. If chilling for more than 1 hour, cover the sheet pan with plastic wrap so the dough doesn't dry out.)

5 Adjust one oven rack to the upper-middle position and another to the lower-middle position. Preheat the oven to 375°F.

6 Grate some of the aged Gouda over each galette. Use a fork to beat the egg with a pinch of salt and 1 tablespoon of water, then use a pastry brush to lightly coat the crust of each galette with the egg wash. Bake until the crust is golden and the apples are tender, 35 to 40 minutes. Serve warm or cooled.

The galettes are best eaten within 1 day of baking; store them at room temperature and warm them in a 325°F oven before serving.

1 tablespoon caraway
seeds

¼ cup apple juice

½ cup dried currants

1¾ cups all-purpose
flour, plus extra for
shaping

3 ounces aged Gouda
cheese, grated on
the medium-hole
side of a box grater
(about 1 cup)

1 tablespoon baking
powder

1 tablespoon sugar

½ teaspoon plus a
pinch of kosher salt

4 tablespoons (½ stick)
cold unsalted butter,
cut into small pieces

⅔ cup heavy (whipping)
cream

1 large egg

AGED GOUDA, CARAWAY, AND CURRANT SCONES

I first tasted this intriguing combination of flavors at New York Times *columnist Melissa Clark's house. Mine are a bit different than hers—she adds onions and rye flour while I instead mix in nutty, butterscotch-y Gouda cheese. Fluffy, rich, and so sweet-savory, these scones are spectacular for breakfast or at dinner instead of bread or a roll.*

1 Line a rimmed sheet pan with parchment paper or a nonstick baking mat and set aside.

2 Place the caraway seeds in a small skillet set over medium heat and toast, shaking the pan often, until the seeds are fragrant and wisps of smoke rise off the surface, 1½ to 2 minutes. Transfer the seeds to a small plate.

3 Add the apple juice to the skillet and bring it to a simmer; turn off the heat. Place the currants in a small bowl, then pour in the warm apple juice. Cover with plastic wrap and set aside to plump for 15 minutes, then drain off any liquid.

4 Place the flour, ½ cup of the cheese, baking powder, sugar, toasted caraway seeds, and ½ teaspoon of the salt in the bowl of a food processor and pulse for five 1-second pulses to combine (or whisk in a large bowl to combine—place the caraway seeds in a ziplock bag and crush them with a heavy pot before using, if you like). Add the butter and pulse for five 1-second pulses, then add the currants and pulse five more times. With the processor running, add the heavy cream; process to combine, about six 1-second pulses.

5 Lightly flour your work surface and turn the dough out onto it. Press and knead the dough for ten to twelve strokes. Pat the dough into an 8-inch circle that's about ¾ inch thick. Whisk the egg, 1 tablespoon of water, and a pinch of salt together in a small bowl. Brush the egg wash over the dough and sprinkle with the remaining ¼ cup of cheese. Cut the circle into eight equal wedges (like a pie). Separate the pieces and set them 1 inch apart on the prepared sheet pan (closer together if you like softer edges). Cover and chill for 30 minutes or up to overnight.

6 Preheat the oven to 375°F. Remove the scones from the refrigerator and uncover.

7 Bake until the scones are golden, about 20 minutes. Serve warm or at room temperature.

The scones are at their very best within a few hours of baking, but will keep, in an airtight container at room temperature, for up to 3 days. Warm them in a 250°F oven before serving.

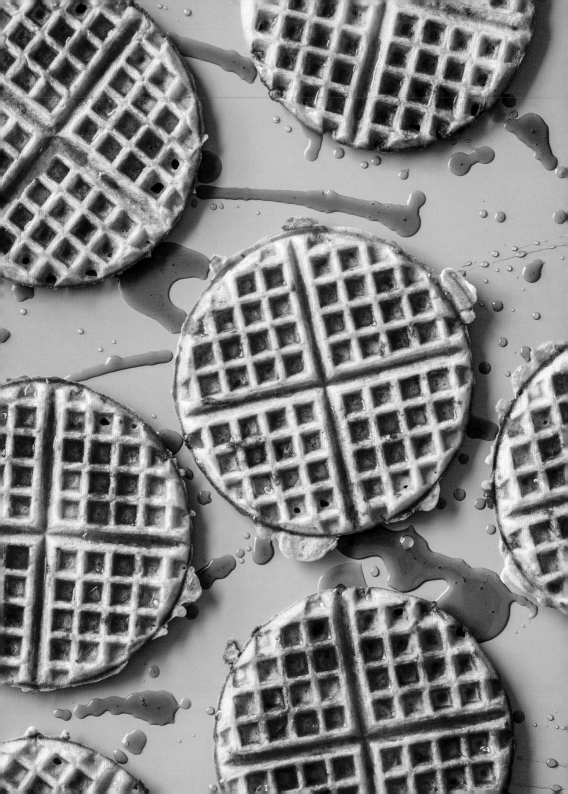

CRISPY CHEDDAR CHEESE WAFFLES

MAKES 8 ROUND, THIN WAFFLES

UMAMI BOMBS:

1½ cups all-purpose flour

½ cup sweet rice flour (see Note)

½ cup cornstarch

2 tablespoons sugar

1 teaspoon baking powder

1 teaspoon baking soda

2 teaspoons kosher salt

2 cups buttermilk

2 large eggs, separated

2 teaspoons pure vanilla extract

10 tablespoons (1¼ sticks) unsalted butter, melted, plus cold butter for serving (optional)

3 ounces sharp Cheddar cheese, grated on the medium-hole side of a box grater (about 1 cup)

Nonstick cooking spray

Warm maple syrup, for serving

One question I always get asked when I write a cookbook is this: "What's your favorite recipe?" And I always end up saying something like this: "Oh, it's so hard to choose, there are so many great ones. . . ." Well, you want to know a secret? This is my favorite recipe in the book. It's sweet and savory, the cheese gets crispy-salty-crunchy, the waffles are crisp-tender (thank you, rice flour and cornstarch, and, yes, crisp-tender can exist in the world of textural opposites), and with maple syrup poured over the top, I'm just in heaven. And hey, please warm that maple syrup before serving! It's the little things that make life sweet. (Note: I think these waffles turn out best when made in a thin, shallow waffle maker.)

1 Whisk the flour, rice flour, cornstarch, 1 tablespoon of the sugar, baking powder, baking soda, and salt together in a large bowl. Preheat a waffle iron according to the manufacturer's instructions. Set a sheet pan in the oven and preheat it to 250°F.

>>

2 Whisk the buttermilk, egg yolks, and vanilla together in a medium bowl. In a separate medium bowl (or the bowl of a stand mixer fitted with the whip attachment), beat the egg whites with the remaining 1 tablespoon of sugar until the whites hold stiff peaks.

3 Add the buttermilk mixture to the flour mixture, pour in the melted butter, add the cheese, and stir to combine. Use a whisk or rubber spatula to fold in the egg whites.

4 Spray the waffle iron with nonstick cooking spray and then add enough batter to fill the waffle mold about two-thirds of the way to the edge. Close the waffle maker and cook until the waffle is browned and crisp. Transfer the waffle to the sheet pan, cover with a kitchen towel, and keep warm in the oven while you make the rest of the waffles. Serve immediately with more butter (if you like) and warm maple syrup.

NOTE: *Sweet rice flour is ground short-grain sweet rice. It's available in most health food stores and online. I use Bob's Red Mill brand.*

7 tablespoons unsalted butter, at room temperature

4 scallions, trimmed, white and light green parts thinly sliced

2 garlic cloves, peeled and thinly sliced

¼ teaspoon freshly ground black pepper

7 large eggs

1½ cups (4 to 5 ounces) finely grated aged Gouda cheese (preferably grated using a rasp-style grater)

½ teaspoon kosher salt

¼ cup whole milk, heavy (whipping) cream, or half-and-half

¼ cup finely chopped fresh dill

GOUDA-DILL FRITTATA
WITH BROWNED BUTTER

This is a brunch party winner. Have the eggs and grated Gouda already whisked up in a bowl, and then, when your guests arrive, stir in the browned butter–scallion mixture and milk and pour into the buttered baking dish. By the time everyone is seated, the frittata will be puffed up perfectly and ready for its entrance.

1 Adjust an oven rack to the lower-middle position. Preheat the oven to 375°F. Grease a 2-quart baking dish or oven-safe skillet with 1 tablespoon of the butter and set aside.

2 Melt the remaining 6 tablespoons butter in a small saucepan over medium-high heat, then reduce the heat to medium. Add the scallions, garlic, and black pepper and cook, swirling often, until the butter is nutty-brown and fragrant, 6 to 8 minutes.

3 Crack the eggs into a large bowl and whisk in the Gouda, salt, and milk. Whisk in the scallion butter and pour the mixture into the prepared baking dish. Place it in the oven and bake until puffed and golden and the center resists light pressure, 22 to 25 minutes. Remove from the oven, sprinkle with the dill, and serve immediately.

CHEDDAR CORNBREAD

- 2¼ cups all-purpose flour
- 1 cup fine cornmeal
- 1 cup sugar
- 2 tablespoons plus ½ teaspoon baking powder
- 1 tablespoon kosher salt
- ¼ teaspoon freshly ground black pepper
- ¼ cup pureed silken tofu (see Note)
- 3 tablespoons flaxseeds, finely ground (or 2½ tablespoons flax meal)
- 1½ cups whole milk
- 2 teaspoons distilled white vinegar
- 6 tablespoons coconut oil, liquefied
- 6 tablespoons (¾ stick) unsalted butter, melted, plus 1 tablespoon for greasing the pan
- 3 ounces sharp Cheddar cheese, grated on the medium-hole side of a box grater (about 1 cup)

The sharpness of the Cheddar plays off the sweetness of the coconut oil, but also adds critical umami to this fluffy, light, and very, very tasty cornbread. I also sometimes add chopped jalapeños, scallions, and cilantro, which make it herby and kind of spicy (in a good way). The tofu and flaxseeds give it extra protein and nutrients.

1 Adjust an oven rack to the middle position and preheat the oven to 425°F.

2 Whisk together the flour, cornmeal, sugar, baking powder, salt, and pepper in a medium bowl.

3 Whisk together the pureed tofu, ground flaxseeds, and milk in a large bowl. Place a 12-inch oven-safe skillet (preferably cast-iron) or a 2-quart casserole dish in the oven.

4 Whisk the vinegar into the tofu mixture, then add the flour mixture, coconut oil, and 6 tablespoons melted butter. Stir until nearly combined, then add the cheese and stir until incorporated.

NOTE: *Pureed tofu couldn't be simpler to make: Place the silken tofu in a blender and buzz it until smooth. You can also use the small bowl attachment of a food processor.*

5 Place the remaining 1 tablespoon of butter in the skillet in the oven and let it warm up and sizzle for 2 minutes. Then carefully remove the skillet, tilt it to spread the butter around, and pour the cornbread batter into it. Spread it out evenly with a silicone spatula and quickly get the pan back in the oven.

6 Bake until the cornbread is golden brown, resists light pressure, and a cake tester comes out with just a crumb or two attached, about 30 minutes. Remove from the oven and let cool slightly, then slice into wedges and serve warm or at room temperature.

The cornbread will keep, covered at room temperature, for up to 3 days.

CHAPTER

FERMENTED, MUSHROOMY, CARAMELY

As with wine, when you have a great soy sauce, you can just tell. It isn't tinny, it isn't *salty*. It's just. So. Good. It's round and sweet and has a mushroomy, fermented quality that is almost like sherry. Now, add a splash of this magical liquid to, say, tomato sauce for a ragu, or to sautéed greens, or even to the chocolate frosting for chocolate cake, and you have something that just tastes a little brighter and a little more colorful. And don't worry, your chocolate cake isn't going to taste like soy sauce—I swear!

Soy sauce, first made about 2,500 years ago, is loaded with glutamates, the amino acids that give it its long, savory notes. Made by fermenting a mash of wheat (or barley or rice) with soybeans, salt, and yeast (this mash is called *koji*), it can be aged for years for a super lush and nuanced taste, or on the other hand, the ingredients can be manipulated to achieve a similar flavor in just a few days if chemicals and artificial flavors are added.

My soy sauce of choice is Japanese shoyu or tamari, which are naturally fermented and a little less salty than their Chinese counterpart (and, in the case of tamari, is wheat free).

SERVES 6

UMAMI BOMBS:

2 cups dry red wine

⅔ cup soy sauce

Kosher salt

2 packages (8 to 9 ounces each) soba noodles

1 block firm tofu (12 to 14 ounces), drained, patted dry, sliced into ¼-inch-thick slabs, then into bite-size pieces

2 tablespoons plus 1½ teaspoons toasted (dark) sesame oil

1 medium cucumber, peeled and sliced into long, thin strips (scoop out the seeds first, if they're large)

1 large red or orange bell pepper, halved, seeded, and sliced into long, thin strips

1 jalapeño, stemmed and sliced crosswise into thin rounds (optional; seed the jalapeño to make it less spicy)

4 scallions, trimmed, white and green parts thinly sliced on a diagonal

SOBA SALAD
WITH SOY-RED WINE REDUCTION

Reducing red wine over low-and-slow heat on the stovetop intensifies its flavor and sweetness. Adding soy sauce to the pan adds a deep savory note, and a splash of toasted sesame oil complements the heartiness of buckwheat soba noodles. This is an ideal make-ahead salad—toss everything together several hours before serving, saving the sesame seeds and herbs for sprinkling just before you set the salad on the table.

1 Combine the red wine, soy sauce, and ½ teaspoon of salt in a medium saucepan and bring to a simmer over medium-high heat. Reduce the heat to medium-low and simmer very gently (with just a couple of bubbles popping at the surface) until the mixture is reduced to ½ cup, 15 to 20 minutes. Turn off the heat and set aside.

2 Bring a large pot of water to a boil. Add 1 tablespoon of salt and the soba noodles and boil according to the package instructions until the soba is tender. Drain through a fine-mesh sieve and rinse the soba under cold water to cool it down. Set aside.

2 medium garlic cloves, peeled and grated or minced

2-inch piece fresh ginger, peeled and grated or minced

2 tablespoons rice wine

Juice of 1 lime

3 tablespoons toasted sesame seeds (see box)

1 cup packed fresh herbs (basil, cilantro, mint, or a combination), finely chopped or torn

3 Adjust an oven rack to the top position and heat the broiler to high. Line a sheet pan with parchment paper. Set the tofu on the prepared pan and drizzle with 1½ teaspoons of the oil, then sprinkle with a few pinches of salt. Broil the tofu until browned, 8 to 10 minutes (watch the tofu closely, as broiler intensities vary). Remove from the broiler and set aside.

4 Place the cucumber, bell pepper, jalapeño, scallions, garlic, ginger, rice wine, lime juice, and 2 teaspoons of salt in a medium bowl and toss to combine.

5 Place the cooled soba noodles in a large bowl. Add the red wine sauce and the remaining 2 tablespoons of oil and stir to coat. Top with the vegetables, then sprinkle with the sesame seeds and herbs, and serve.

The soba salad will keep, in an airtight container in the refrigerator, for up to 8 hours.

TOASTING SEEDS AND NUTS

Place the seeds or nuts in a small skillet (preferably stainless steel or cast-iron—since you're toasting them in a dry pan, it's best not to use nonstick) and toast them over medium heat, shaking the pan often, until golden brown, 2 to 3 minutes for seeds, and a bit longer for nuts. Keep an eye on them because they can burn easily. Transfer to a plate to cool before using.

WHAT KIND OF SOY SAUCE SHOULD YOU BUY?

Generally speaking, soy sauce can be purchased "light" or "dark." The light soy sauce found in China is what most Americans are used to flavor-wise, with dark soy sauce usually having a thicker and more syrupy consistency (sometimes molasses is even added to achieve its signature heftier body). In Japan, dark soy sauce is richer in flavor but less salty as well—this is the kind of soy sauce I keep in my kitchen. Japanese soy sauce is lighter in flavor and sweeter than Chinese soy sauce. (I like Japanese soy sauce called shoyu or tamari, which is wheat-free.)

ADD A SPLASH OF SOY

Here are some other fun ways to bring soy sauce into a dish for just a little oomph. A couple of things to remember: Soy sauce is salty, so use restraint when adding it to a dish (you may want to reduce the amount of kosher or sea salt used). Also, soy sauce is dark and will make whatever you're adding it to a little darker (unless it's a large pot of something). Try soy splashed into . . .

>> a balsamic or red wine vinaigrette

>> red wine before deglazing a pan to make a pan sauce

>> a pot of soup, chili, or hearty stew

>> a marinade

>> almost anything with chocolate—chocolate pudding, chocolate ice cream base, hot fudge sauce . . .

MAKES 2 CUPS
UMAMI BOMBS: ●●

- 2 tablespoons extra-virgin olive oil
- 3 garlic cloves, peeled and minced
- 6 fresh basil leaves, roughly torn
- Pinch of crushed red pepper flakes
- 1 box (26.5 ounces) tomato puree
- 1 tablespoon soy sauce
- 1 teaspoon kosher salt

SIMPLE SOY MARINARA

Does the world really need another marinara sauce? Um, yes! Especially when a little soy is splashed in for umami and depth. When buying canned, jarred, or boxed tomatoes, be sure to look at the nutrition panel to make sure they aren't loaded with salt or sugar (compare the back panel to that of one with no salt or added sugar and see how they differ). You can use this marinara in place of any marinara for any recipe.

---

1 Heat the oil with the garlic in a large skillet over medium-high heat. Once the garlic starts to sizzle, add the basil and crushed red pepper flakes and continue to cook, stirring often, until the garlic is golden, 30 seconds to 1 minute.

2 Add the tomato puree, soy sauce, and salt, reduce the heat to medium-low, and cook, stirring often, for 2 minutes.

3 Taste and add more salt if needed, then turn off the heat and set aside to cool.

The sauce will keep, in an airtight container in the refrigerator, for up to 1 week.

EGGS IN PUTTANESCA PURGATORY

2 tablespoons extra-virgin olive oil, plus extra for serving

3 tablespoons capers (rinsed if salt-packed)

½ teaspoon crushed red pepper flakes

¼ cup pitted and roughly chopped oil-cured black olives

2 cups Simple Soy Marinara (page 52) or your favorite store-bought marinara

2 tablespoons roughly chopped flat-leaf parsley or basil leaves

4 large eggs

Flaky salt, for garnish

Grated Parmigiano-Reggiano cheese, for garnish (optional)

Toasted or grilled bread, buttered or brushed with olive oil, for serving

There's just no way to say it politely—alla puttanesca roughly translates to "in the style of the whore." Maybe because the sauce is sultry, spicy, briny, and absolutely overwhelmed with umami characteristics. The eggs are baked suspended in this sauce—what tastier limbo in which to seek absolution of their sins?

1 Heat the oil in a large, deep nonstick skillet over medium-high heat. Add the capers and crushed red pepper flakes and cook, stirring occasionally, until the capers get a little crisp, about 2 minutes.

2 Add the olives, and once they start to sizzle, stir in the marinara sauce and bring it to a simmer. Reduce the heat to medium-low and stir in the parsley or basil.

3 Use a spoon to make a well in the sauce (as best you can) and crack an egg into it. Repeat with the remaining eggs. Cover and cook until the whites are set but the yolks are runny, 4 to 6 minutes.

4 Divide between two or four bowls. Sprinkle with salt, olive oil, and cheese (if using) and serve immediately with toast.

V

SERVES 4

UMAMI BOMBS: ✦

▬▬▬▬▬▬▬▬▬▬

¼ cup extra-virgin
olive oil

5 garlic cloves, peeled
and thinly sliced

1 teaspoon freshly
ground black pepper

1 teaspoon crushed
red pepper flakes

2 bunches kale,
tough stems
removed, leaves
roughly chopped
(about 12 cups)

6 cups baby spinach

2 teaspoons kosher salt

1 tablespoon plus
1 teaspoon soy sauce

UMAMI GREENS
WITH GARLIC AND SOY

*These quick-sautéed greens are a total savior. I'll
often cook them up (any combo of kale, spinach,
broccoli rabe, Swiss chard) and pile them on top of a
slice (yes, pizza!). My kids have gotten into this habit,
too, sometimes "greening" a slice, and sometimes just
eating the greens on the side. If you have fewer greens
than the amount called for, halve the recipe—it works
just as beautifully.*

▬▬▬▬▬▬▬▬▬▬

1 Combine the oil, garlic, black pepper, and crushed
red pepper flakes in a large skillet over medium
heat. Stir occasionally until the garlic becomes
fragrant and golden, about 1½ minutes.

2 Stir in half of the kale. After 1 to 2 minutes, the
kale will begin to wilt. Add the remaining kale,
using tongs and a wooden spoon to turn the fresh kale
into the wilted kale until, after another 2 minutes or
so, two-thirds of the greens are wilted.

3 Add the spinach, salt, and soy sauce and use the
tongs and the spoon to lift and turn the spinach into
the rest of the greens. Cook just until the spinach wilts,
about 1 minute. Taste for seasoning and then transfer to
a serving bowl. Serve warm or at room temperature.

The greens will keep, in an airtight container in the
refrigerator, for 2 days.

SERVES 4

UMAMI BOMBS:

1 tablespoon kosher
salt

1 pound Brussels sprouts,
ends trimmed and
halved lengthwise

2 tablespoons soy sauce

1 tablespoon sambal
oelek

1 tablespoon honey
or maple syrup
(see Note)

2 teaspoons toasted
(dark) sesame oil

2 medium garlic cloves,
peeled and grated on
a rasp-style grater
or minced

1-inch piece fresh
ginger, peeled and
grated or minced

1 tablespoon grapeseed
or canola oil

Flaky sea salt,
for garnish

¼ cup roughly chopped
roasted and salted
peanuts

Finely chopped fresh
herbs (basil, cilantro,
mint, or a combination)

SHEET PAN CHILE-SOY GLAZED BRUSSELS SPROUTS

My go-to Brussels sprouts dish used to be halved Brussels tossed in olive oil and then hot-roasted on a sheet pan with bacon and red onions until caramelized, crisped, smoky, and bathed in bacon fat. Now, well, I have a healthier and more Earth-kind option: homemade chile-soy sauce. It's smoky and a little spicy, and it has a lot of umami going on. It's not bacon—it's better. You can find sambal oelek, an Asian chile-garlic sauce, in the international aisle of most supermarkets—if it's not there, sub in sriracha.

1 Adjust one oven rack to the upper-middle position and another to the middle position. Set a rimmed sheet pan on the middle oven rack and preheat the oven to 425°F.

2 Bring a medium pot of water to a boil over high heat and add the kosher salt. Add the Brussels sprouts and boil until bright green and just starting to get tender, about 5 minutes, then drain in a colander or fine-mesh sieve and run under cold water to stop the cooking.

3 Whisk together the soy sauce, sambal oelek, honey, sesame oil, garlic, and ginger in a large bowl and set aside.

4 Remove the sheet pan from the oven, add the grapeseed oil and tilt the pan to coat, then quickly turn the Brussels sprouts out onto the pan and give the pan a quick shake to spread them out. Return to the oven and cook until the sprouts are browned and tender, 15 to 20 minutes.

5 Carefully remove the pan from the oven and transfer the Brussels sprouts to the bowl with the chile-soy mixture, tossing to combine. Return the sprouts to the sheet pan, shaking the pan to spread them out. Turn the broiler on high, place the sheet pan on the upper rack, and broil just until the glaze starts to sizzle, about 2 minutes (watch the sprouts closely, as broiler intensities vary).

6 Transfer the Brussels sprouts to a platter, sprinkle with sea salt, peanuts, and herbs, and serve.

The Brussels sprouts will keep, in an airtight container in the refrigerator, for up to 3 days.

NOTE: *To make this vegan, use maple syrup instead of honey.*

VO

SERVES 2 OR 3
(OR DOUBLE TO SERVE 4 OR 6)
UMAMI BOMBS: 🖌🖌

¼ cup soy sauce

2 tablespoons rice wine

2 teaspoons toasted
(dark) sesame oil

2 tablespoons
grapeseed or
canola oil

3 to 4 scallions,
trimmed, white and
green parts finely
chopped

1 red bell pepper,
halved, seeded,
and finely chopped

1-inch piece fresh
ginger, peeled and
grated

2 medium garlic cloves,
peeled and grated
on a rasp or minced

¼ teaspoon kosher salt

1 cup frozen shelled
edamame (or frozen
or fresh green peas)

2 large eggs, lightly
beaten (optional)

2½ to 3 cups cooked
white or brown rice,
refrigerated or at
room temperature
(see Note)

FRIED RICE
WITH RED PEPPERS,
EDAMAME, AND SCALLIONS

*My hands-down favorite weekday breakfast to make
for my kids is fried rice—and when I have leftover
cooked rice in the fridge, it all comes together in about
15 minutes. It makes me so very happy to know they're
getting an awesome, hearty, savory meal in their bellies
before I send them off to school—I know they'll be able
to focus and stay on point until lunchtime. Feel free to
add any and all vegetables you like to this dish. Omit
the egg for a vegan version.*

1 Measure the soy sauce in a liquid measuring
cup, then add the rice wine and sesame oil and
set aside.

2 Heat the grapeseed oil in a large nonstick skillet
over medium-high heat. Add the scallions, red
pepper, ginger, garlic, and salt and cook, stirring
often, until the ginger and garlic are fragrant, 1 to 2
minutes. Stir in the edamame and cook for 1 minute.

3 Add the eggs, if using, and stir around until they
are nearly set, 1 to 1½ minutes, then pour in
the soy sauce mixture. It should come to a simmer

quickly. Stir in the rice and let it cook, without stirring, to get it nice and hot and even a little browned along the bottom, about 2 minutes. Then, give the fried rice a stir to distribute everything. Divide it among bowls, and serve immediately.

The fried rice will keep, in an airtight container in the refrigerator, for about 3 days.

NOTE: *Fried rice is best made with rice that either has been refrigerated for a few hours or is at room temperature; the best way to bring hot rice to room temperature is to spread it out on a rimmed sheet pan and let it cool completely.*

KILLER CHOCOLATE CAKE

FOR THE CAKE

1 cup (2 sticks) plus
   1 tablespoon unsalted
   butter, at room
   temperature

2⅓ cups all-purpose
   flour

½ cup Dutch-process
   cocoa powder

1½ teaspoons baking
   powder

½ teaspoon baking
   soda

½ teaspoon fine
   sea salt

1¾ cups buttermilk

2 teaspoons pure
   vanilla extract

2¼ cups light brown
   sugar

3 large eggs

8 ounces semisweet or
   bittersweet chocolate,
   finely chopped, and
   melted (see Note)

This is your all-purpose, everyday, no-reason, intensely chocolatey, take-a-sliver-every-time-you-pass-it chocolate cake. Moist and rich, the true secret ingredient here is the soy sauce in the frosting. FOR REAL. It adds just a little salty note that really pulls the cake together. I dare you not to love it at first bite. Just ask my editor.

1 *Make the cake:* Preheat the oven to 350°F. Grease a 9-by-13-inch glass or metal cake pan with the 1 tablespoon of room temperature butter.

2 Whisk together the flour, cocoa, baking powder, baking soda, and salt in a large bowl. Combine the buttermilk and vanilla in a medium bowl or a 2-cup liquid measuring cup.

3 In the bowl of a stand mixer fitted with the paddle attachment (or in a large bowl, if using a handheld mixer), cream the 1 cup of butter and the brown sugar on low speed until creamy and well combined. Increase the speed to medium-high and beat until light and airy, about 2 minutes. Reduce the mixer speed to medium-low and add the eggs one at a time, mixing well between each addition and

FOR THE FROSTING

- 10 tablespoons (1¼ sticks) unsalted butter, at room temperature
- 1 cup confectioners' sugar
- 4 ounces bittersweet chocolate, finely chopped, melted, and cooled to room temperature (see Note)
- 2 tablespoons soy sauce
- 1 teaspoon pure vanilla extract

scraping down the side and bottom of the bowl as needed. Once all 3 eggs are added, beat for 1 minute on medium speed to get the mixture nice and fluffy.

4 Reduce the speed to medium-low and add the flour mixture alternately with the buttermilk mixture in three batches, starting with the flour. Add the melted chocolate and mix on medium speed until well incorporated, stopping the mixer to scrape down the side and bottom of the bowl as needed.

5 Use a rubber or offset spatula to scrape the batter into the prepared pan and even it out as much as possible. Bake until a cake tester inserted into the center of the cake comes out clean and the center of the cake resists light pressure, about 40 minutes. Remove from the oven and set aside to cool completely, at least 2 hours, before frosting.

6 *Make the frosting:* Put the butter in the bowl of a stand mixer fitted with the whisk attachment (or in a medium bowl, if using a handheld mixer). Beat on medium-high speed until smooth. Turn off the mixer and sift the confectioners' sugar into the bowl and combine on low speed. Add the melted chocolate, soy sauce, and vanilla and beat on low speed until combined. Increase the mixer speed to medium-low and whip until glossy, 15 to 30 seconds.

7 Use an offset spatula or butter knife to spread the frosting on top of the cooled cake. Cut into squares and serve.

The cake will keep, loosely covered with plastic wrap in the refrigerator, for up to 3 days. Let it sit out at room temperature for 15 to 20 minutes before slicing and serving.

NOTE: *There are a few simple ways to go about melting chocolate. Most often, I resort to the microwave—simply place finely chopped chocolate in a microwave-safe bowl and microwave it on high in 20-second increments, stirring between each one, until the chocolate is melted. Or you can use a bain marie (water bath): Fill a medium saucepan with water to a depth of 1 inch and bring to a simmer over high heat. Turn the heat down to medium-low and place the finely chopped chocolate in a heat-safe metal bowl set atop the pot. Stir the chocolate every 30 seconds to 1 minute until it is melted. (Be sure the bottom of the bowl doesn't touch the simmering water, or the chocolate could scorch and turn pasty.)*

2¼ cups old-fashioned (rolled) oats

½ cup shredded unsweetened coconut

¼ cup sesame seeds

2 tablespoons toasted (dark) sesame oil

2 tablespoons sugar (preferably unrefined cane sugar)

2 tablespoons soy sauce

Finely grated zest of 1 medium orange

1½ teaspoons peeled and grated fresh ginger

1½ teaspoons ground coriander

½ teaspoon ground ginger

¼ teaspoon ground cinnamon (ideally smoked cinnamon; see Note)

Flaky salt, for garnish

TOASTED SESAME GRANOLA
WITH COCONUT, ORANGE, AND WARM SPICES

Simple, a little salty, a little smoky, a little citrus-and-spicy, this granola is great over yogurt or chocolate ice cream. I also like to eat it with warm almond milk in the winter, kind of like a morning porridge. Unrefined cane sugar has a pale brown color and coarse texture—almost like Demerara sugar. Because the sugar is unrefined, it retains some of the molasses flavor and tint that would otherwise be removed during processing. I think the flavor adds to the overall tastiness of the granola. Feel free to get creative, too—I was at a friend's place in the country and we baked the granola in her outdoor wood oven. The smoky/woodsy flavor was phenomenal!

1 Preheat the oven to 350°F. Line a rimmed sheet pan with parchment paper or a nonstick baking mat and set aside.

2 Toss the oats, coconut, sesame seeds, and oil together in a large bowl, making sure everything gets nicely coated with the oil. Spread the mixture in an even layer onto the prepared sheet pan (don't clean the bowl, you'll use it again in Step 3). Toast in the oven until lightly golden, 6 to 7 minutes.

3 Whisk the sugar, soy sauce, orange zest, fresh ginger, coriander, ground ginger, and cinnamon together in the bowl you used for the oats.

4 Use the parchment to lift the oat mixture off the sheet pan and transfer it to the bowl with the sugar mixture. Set the parchment aside. Stir the oat and sugar mixtures to combine, and then return the parchment to the pan and spread the granola on top. Continue to bake until golden brown but not too dark, 8 to 10 minutes. Sprinkle with flaky salt and cool completely.

The granola will keep, in an airtight container at room temperature, for up to 2 weeks.

NOTE: *La Boîte, a spice shop in New York City, sells incredible smoked cinnamon. It's available online, too—laboiteny.com—and will completely transform your oatmeal/granola/pumpkin pie game.*

CHAPTER

SWEET, TART, ACIDIC, CITRUSY

When you think of umami, you might not think of tomatoes, but you should. The combination of acidic, sweet, and savory—specifically glutamic acid—is especially high in tomatoes, and as tomatoes ripen, the amount of glutamates increases as well. Now, cook those tomatoes and you concentrate all of that savory deliciousness, intensifying the sweet along with it—that's what you find in roasted tomatoes and even more so in sun-dried tomatoes. Roasted tomatoes lend themselves particularly well to tarts, salsa, and even tomato butter. I make sun-dried tomatoes into a spreadable vegan pepperoni (for real!) that's a version of the Italian sausage spread 'nduja, and of course tomato soup is always an umami bomb, especially with some grated Parmigiano-Reggiano or aged Gouda sprinkled over the top.

**MAKES 16 HALVES
(ABOUT 2¼ CUPS DEPENDING
ON HOW BIG AND JUICY
YOUR TOMATOES ARE)**

UMAMI BOMBS:

ROASTED TOMATOES

With some roasted tomatoes on hand in the fridge (or freezer), you can save the day. Okay, maybe not like save *the day, but you can certainly make it a lot better since you have what it takes to make tomato soup, salsa, roasted tomato butter (which adds the most wonderful tomato flavor to pan sauces, pasta, and even toast; page 80), and pasta sauce. When the tomatoes concentrate in the oven, their umami qualities become more intense as well, and even winter tomatoes come out sweeter and more intoxicating than they were when fresh. Sometimes I just like to top a piece of toast with some creamy goat's milk cheese or ricotta and place a roasted tomato or two on top. It's my kind of fast food.*

1 tablespoon extra-virgin olive oil

1 teaspoon kosher salt

½ teaspoon garlic powder

¼ teaspoon onion powder

¼ teaspoon crushed red pepper flakes

¼ teaspoon freshly ground black pepper

8 plum tomatoes (about 1¾ pounds), halved lengthwise

1 Preheat the oven to 375°F. Line a rimmed sheet pan with parchment paper or a nonstick baking mat.

2 Stir together the oil, salt, garlic and onion powders, crushed red pepper flakes, and black pepper in a large bowl. Add the tomato halves and toss to combine, coating the tomatoes well with the spice paste.

3 Turn the tomatoes out onto the prepared sheet pan and place them cut side up. Roast until they are very soft, tender, and a little shriveled,

40 minutes to 1 hour, depending on the ripeness of your tomatoes (less-ripe tomatoes will take closer to 1 hour, sometimes a few minutes longer than that).

4 Remove the tomatoes from the oven and set aside to cool completely.

The roasted tomatoes will keep, in an airtight container in the refrigerator, for up to 1 week.

MORE WAYS TO USE ROASTED TOMATOES

>> **Chop up and sprinkle over avocado toast.**

>> **Puree with garlic, pine nuts, olive oil, and Parm for a roasted tomato pesto.**

>> **Thinly slice and add to a grilled cheese.**

>> **Finely chop and stir in minced onion, jalapeño, and cilantro for salsa.**

>> **Slice and add to pasta tossed with garlic and oil.**

ROASTED TOMATO TART

WITH PESTO AND GOAT'S MILK CHEESE

**SERVES 2 TO 4
(OR MORE FOR A SNACK)**

UMAMI BOMBS:

---

1 sheet (12 to 14 ounces) store-bought puff pastry, thawed in the refrigerator overnight

Flour, for rolling out the pastry

4 ounces aged Gouda cheese

1 large egg

Kosher salt

2 ounces fresh goat's milk cheese

¼ cup store-bought or homemade basil pesto (for an extra umami bomb, try kale pesto on page 215)

8 to 10 halves Roasted Tomatoes (from 4 to 5 whole tomatoes depending on their size; page 74)

Freshly ground black pepper

Frozen puff pastry is flaky, delicate, and, best yet, you can buy it at nearly any grocery store. For this easy-to-assemble tart, it creates a simple base for an herby pesto (traditional basil pesto is fantastic, as is walnut pesto, broccoli pesto, roasted pepper pesto . . .), topped with goat's milk cheese and sweet umami-rich roasted tomatoes. A little aged Gouda gets sprinkled over the dough, too, to give it a little extra flavor. All-butter puff pastry makes all the difference in a tart like this, so be sure to look at the ingredients before purchasing. Start here, then try puff pastry as a stand-in for apple pie crust, quiche crust, and even pizza dough! This tart is an ideal bring-along for picnics.

---

1 Preheat the oven to 425°F. Line a rimmed sheet pan with parchment paper or a nonstick baking mat.

2 Unfold the puff pastry and place it on a lightly floured work surface. Roll the pastry to a ¼-inch-thick rectangle (dust the rolling pin with a little flour if needed). Gently transfer the pastry to the prepared pan and place it in the fridge

»

(or freezer) to chill while you prepare the other ingredients.

3 Grate the Gouda on the medium-hole side of a box grater and set aside. Crack the egg into a small bowl, add 1 teaspoon of water and a pinch of salt, and whisk together. Crumble the goat's milk cheese into another small bowl and set aside.

4 Remove the sheet pan with the puff pastry from the refrigerator. Use a fork to prick the dough all over, then use a pastry brush to lightly coat the entire surface of the pastry with the beaten egg mixture (you may have some left over). Sprinkle the Gouda cheese evenly over the dough and press it down, then fold over the edges of the dough to create a ¾- to 1-inch rim around the pastry.

5 Spread the pesto over the dough (leave the rim bare) and top with the roasted tomato halves, cut side up. Sprinkle with the goat's milk cheese and then with a few pinches of salt and some black pepper. Use any remaining egg wash to brush the edges of the pastry.

6 Bake the tart until it is golden brown around the edges and on the bottom (lift up a corner with a metal spatula to take a peek), 12 to 14 minutes. Remove from the oven and let cool for at least 10 minutes before slicing and serving. The tart is great warm or at room temperature; it is best eaten within a few hours after baking.

1 cup (2 sticks) unsalted butter, at room temperature and mashed with a fork

6 halves Roasted Tomatoes (from 3 whole tomatoes; page 74), finely chopped and then mashed with a fork into a semi-smooth paste

A few pinches of flaky salt

ROASTED TOMATO BUTTER

Flavored butters are so rad. Did you know all you need to make one is softened butter and a seasoning? Anything from citrus zest to roasted garlic, herbs, or even caramelized onions (see Chapter 5) can be chopped up super fine and stirred into butter—roasted tomatoes add a wonderful sweet depth. Try a generous pat of this on roasted vegetables or use it to enrich a pan sauce. It's extra delicious in the Breakfast Pasta on page 12 and the Miso Cacio e Pepe on page 171!

1 Place the mashed butter in a medium bowl, add the mashed tomatoes, and stir until well combined. Add the salt and stir to combine.

2 Place a piece of parchment paper or plastic wrap on your work surface and scrape half of the butter onto the center of the sheet. Use the paper (or plastic) to roll and shape the butter into a 1-inch-wide cylinder. Wrap it well and refrigerate it. Repeat with the remaining butter.

3 Let the butter chill for at least 30 minutes before using, or for 2 hours if you prefer it firm.

The butter will keep, wrapped in the refrigerator, for 5 days.

MAKES 1 CUP
UMAMI BOMBS:

6 halves Roasted
   Tomatoes (from
   3 whole tomatoes;
   page 74), finely
   chopped

1 tablespoon fresh lime
   juice, plus extra as
   needed

1 tablespoon finely
   chopped red onion
   or scallion

1 small jalapeño,
   stemmed and finely
   chopped (seeded
   for less heat)

1 tablespoon finely
   chopped fresh
   cilantro

½ teaspoon kosher salt,
   plus extra as needed

ROASTED TOMATO SALSA

Fresh pico de gallo made with tomatoes, a little onion, jalapeño, and cilantro is awesome when your tomatoes are summer-ripe and at peak sweetness. But if you think I'm limiting my salsa intake to summer and its peak-season tomatoes, then you just don't get me at all. Roast tomatoes and chop them up fine for a killer tomato salsa that is extra satisfying—especially in January when you need a little hot and spicy in your life.

Mix the chopped tomatoes, lime juice, onion, jalapeño, cilantro, and salt together in a medium bowl. Taste and adjust with more salt or lime juice if needed. Serve immediately or refrigerate until ready to use.

The salsa will keep, in an airtight container in the refrigerator, for up to 5 days (the flavors will become stronger the longer the salsa sits).

- 6 tablespoons extra-virgin olive oil

- 1 pound dried spaghettini, broken lengthwise into thirds

- 2 medium yellow onions, peeled, quartered, and thinly sliced crosswise

- 1 cup sun-dried tomatoes (if oil-packed, drain first; if they are very dry or firm, rehydrate them in warm water for 10 minutes before draining and using), finely chopped

- 3 garlic cloves, peeled and minced

- 2 teaspoons finely chopped fresh rosemary

- 1½ teaspoons smoked paprika

- 1¼ teaspoons ground cumin

- 2 teaspoons kosher salt

- ¾ teaspoon freshly ground black pepper

- ¾ cup dry white wine

- ½ cup finely chopped fresh cilantro, for garnish

FIDEOS
WITH SUN-DRIED TOMATOES, CARAMELIZED ONION, AND CILANTRO

Can I make a true confession here? Just between us . . . I love Rice-A-Roni. I mean, does any boxed pilaf have a more perfect texture? And those little bits of vermicelli confetti-ing the whole lot just sends it over the top. In fact, I think this is where my love of fideos (a dish of toasted thin pasta strands popular in Spain and also in some parts of the Middle East) took root. Here, I toast uncooked spaghettini in olive oil to give it that nutty taste, then cook up the rest of the sauce before returning the browned dry pasta to the pan and adding wine, water, and all kinds of spices for it to soak up. Sun-dried tomatoes add umami and make for a twist on pasta marinara that may just hook you.

1 Heat 3 tablespoons of the oil in a large heavy-bottomed pot over medium-high heat for 1 minute. Add the spaghettini and cook, stirring often (using tongs and a wooden spoon together makes turning the pasta much easier), until the strands are brown, 8 to 10 minutes. Transfer the pasta to a large bowl.

2 Put the remaining 3 tablespoons of oil in the pot along with the onions. Cook, stirring occasionally, until the onions begin to fry and sizzle, about 2 minutes. Reduce the heat to medium-low and cook, stirring occasionally, until they are very dark brown and even black in spots, 16 to 20 minutes.

3 Increase the heat to medium-high and stir in the sun-dried tomatoes, garlic, rosemary, paprika, cumin, salt, and pepper and cook, stirring often, until the garlic is fragrant, about 1 minute. Stir in the wine, letting it bubble, and stirring up any browned bits stuck to the bottom of the pot.

4 Increase the heat to high, return the browned pasta to the pot, and stir to coat it with all of the seasonings. Add 4 cups of water, stir, and bring to a boil. Reduce the heat to a gentle simmer, cover the pot, and cook, stirring once or twice, until the pasta is tender and most of the liquid is absorbed, 12 to 15 minutes (if the liquid is absorbed but the pasta isn't al dente yet, add more water, ¼ cup at a time).

5 Divide the fideos among four bowls, sprinkle with cilantro, and serve immediately.

---

2 halves Roasted Tomatoes (from 1 whole tomato; page 74)

⅔ cup mayonnaise or vegan mayonnaise

Kosher salt

8 slices good-quality sandwich bread or squishy commercial bread (your choice—choose wisely)

3 tablespoons extra-virgin olive oil

2 Kirby cucumbers, ends removed, sliced lengthwise into ¼-inch-thick planks

2 medium juicy, ripe tomatoes, stemmed and sliced horizontally into ¼-inch-thick pieces

TOMATO-CUCUMBER SANDWICHES
WITH ROASTED TOMATO MAYO

I learned about the bliss of a tomato-cucumber sandwich from chef David Guas, who has a bakery-restaurant called Bayou Sweet in the DC area. There isn't much to it—a fat, juicy tomato sliced and placed on bread (preferably squishy sandwich slices) with a sweet summer cucumber (best if not refrigerated and fresh from the garden or greenmarket) and lots of mayonnaise—but wow, what a flavor explosion! We were sitting on his porch talking about the book we were working on together (Dam Good Sweet), we got hungry, and he made us these sandwiches. I took a bite and that was it—I was totally hooked. Now, come summertime in NYC, I go to the farmers' market, buy tomatoes and cucumbers, and literally salivate until I get home to make my sandwich. Here, I make it extra umami-y by mashing some roasted tomatoes into the mayo.

---

1 Place the roasted tomatoes on a cutting board and finely chop. Use a fork to smash and mash the tomatoes into a semi-smooth paste, then add the mayonnaise and mix until well combined (if the

mixture looks too runny, add more mayonnaise). Add a pinch of salt and stir to combine. (For a smoother texture, use the small bowl insert of a food processor or a blender or hand mixer; you can also push the mixture through a sieve to eliminate any small bits.)

2 Adjust an oven rack to the top position and heat the broiler to high. Set the bread on a rimmed sheet pan and drizzle with the olive oil. Season with a few pinches of salt. Broil the bread until it is golden brown, 1½ to 2 minutes (watch the bread closely, as broiler intensities vary). Turn the slices over and broil on the other side until golden and dry, 1 to 1½ minutes. Remove the bread from the oven and set one slice on each of four plates, olive oil side up.

3 Spread the bread with some of the tomato mayo, then top with a few cucumber and tomato slices (if you have any leftover mayo, it will keep in the fridge for about a week). Top with the other pieces of bread, olive oil side down. Slice each sandwich in half on a diagonal and serve immediately.

SERVES 4; MAKES 1¼ CUPS
OF MISO BUTTER (YOU'LL HAVE
ABOUT 1 CUP LEFT OVER)

UMAMI BOMBS: ● ●

- 1 cup (2 sticks) unsalted butter, at room temperature and mashed with a fork

- 3 tablespoons miso paste (preferably light-colored miso)

- Vegetable oil, for greasing the grill grates (optional—if using a grill instead of broiler)

- 3 garlic cloves, lightly smashed and peeled

- 4 slices (about ¾ inch thick) crusty, country-style bread

- 1 large juicy, ripe tomato, halved horizontally

- ¼ cup roughly chopped fresh basil leaves, for garnish

- Flaky salt, for garnish

GRILLED PAN CON TOMATE
WITH MISO BUTTER

It sounds awfully fancy, but all this is is a piece of bread with garlic rubbed on it and then a cut tomato smashed and rubbed over that. The bread is toasted so the roughness helps shred the garlic and tomato, luring out its flavor, while the tomato juices simultaneously get sucked up into the bread's interior. What could possibly make this scenario any better? Butter! Miso butter, specifically. The pan con tomate won't taste miso-y, but it will have this wonderful deep, semi-salty funk—i.e., umami—to it that is kind of addictive.

---

1 Place the butter in a medium bowl. Add the miso paste and stir to combine.

2 Adjust an oven rack to the top position and heat the broiler to high, or heat a charcoal or gas grill (or grill pan) to high heat. If using a broiler, line a sheet pan with aluminum foil. If using a grill, brush the hot grill grates with a grill brush. Fold a paper towel into quarters and dip it into the oil, then use long barbecue tongs to grease the grill grates with the oil-saturated towel.

3 Spread some miso butter on one side of each piece of bread. (You will have miso butter leftover—set it aside.) Broil the bread buttered side

up on the prepared pan, or grill it buttered side down, until it is toasted and charred around the edges (broiler) or has grill marks (grill or grill pan), 1½ to 2 minutes (watch the bread closely, as broiler and grill intensities vary). Turn the bread over and broil or grill on the other side until golden and slightly charred, about 1½ minutes more.

4 Set each piece of bread on a plate. Rub the garlic on the buttered side of each slice, followed by the cut side of a tomato half, squeezing the tomato over the bread until you are left with mostly pulp and skin (each tomato half should cover two toasts). Sprinkle the toasts with the basil and flaky salt and serve immediately.

To store the leftover miso butter, place a piece of parchment paper or plastic wrap on your work surface and scrape half of the miso butter onto the center of the sheet. Use the paper (or plastic) to roll and shape the butter into a 1-inch-wide cylinder. Wrap it well and refrigerate it. Repeat with the remaining butter. It will keep, wrapped in the refrigerator, for about 1 week.

MAKES ABOUT 1½ CUPS

UMAMI BOMBS: ✦✦

6 ounces mild green
   olives (choose
   ones that aren't
   too bitter, such
   as Castelvetrano,
   Lucques, or Picholine),
   drained and pitted

1 cup sun-dried tomatoes
   (drained and blotted
   dry if oil-packed)

1½ teaspoons garlic
   powder

1 teaspoon ground
   fennel

¾ teaspoon kosher salt
   or 1 teaspoon smoked
   flaky salt

½ teaspoon smoked
   paprika

½ teaspoon sweet
   paprika

½ teaspoon ground
   cayenne pepper

½ teaspoon freshly
   ground black pepper

Baguette slices,
   for serving

TOMATO 'NDUJA

First, an explanation: Traditional 'nduja (some people say doo-JA like the "JA" in Jamaica; others say en-dew-ya) is like a cross between pepperoni and a spreadable pâté. It's very flavorful, fatty, and unctuous and comes from the south of Italy. My vegan version, made with olives, sun-dried tomatoes, and the usual sausage/ pepperoni flavors of fennel, paprika (both smoked and sweet), and cayenne for heat, comes right close. In fact, I crumbled some over polenta for a vegan friend, and he said, "Wait, is that meat?" and then refused to eat any more. Which I took as a win for the tomato 'nduja and its ability to be a great porky, crumbled sausage-y stand-in to top a pizza or focaccia, stuff a quesadilla, twirl into pasta, or lend anything a bit of meaty funk.

Place the olives on a stack of doubled paper towels and press firmly to dry and press out any juices. Transfer the olives to the bowl of a food processor and add the sun-dried tomatoes, garlic powder, fennel, salt, smoked and sweet paprika, cayenne, and black pepper. Pulverize until well mixed. Taste and add more salt if needed.

The 'nduja will keep, in an airtight container in the refrigerator, for up to 1 week.

2 tablespoons extra-virgin olive oil

1 bunch Swiss chard, tough stems removed and leaves finely chopped (about 4½ cups from 5 large leaves)

1 garlic clove, peeled and minced

½ teaspoon kosher salt

10 ounces dried penne pasta

1 can (28 ounces) crushed tomatoes

2 cups half-and-half

¾ cup finely grated Parmigiano-Reggiano cheese

1 cup ricotta cheese

¼ cup fresh basil leaves, stacked, rolled, and sliced crosswise into ribbons

CREAMY TOMATO PASTA BAKE
WITH SWISS CHARD AND RICOTTA

You don't even have to cook the pasta before baking this dish, making it a great recipe to hand off to an independence-seeking tween or teen who asks for more responsibility in the kitchen but doesn't have the knife skills to rock out a fine mince. Both the Swiss chard and basil can be torn by hand, and the garlic can be pushed through a garlic press or grated on a rasp-style grater (though be wary of little knuckles getting nicked on the sharp teeth!), so you don't even need to worry about knife technique (or lack thereof)—which is good for kids and some adults, too! Oh, and did I mention that this is creamy, cheesy, and loaded with comforting noodles? It is—and it's good.

1 Adjust one oven rack to the top position and another to the middle position. Preheat the oven to 400°F. Coat a 9-by-13-inch baking dish with 1 tablespoon of oil.

2 Place the Swiss chard in a large bowl and add the remaining 1 tablespoon of oil, the garlic,

and ¼ teaspoon of salt. Massage the chard for 20 seconds to incorporate the oil mixture. This will soften the greens and decrease their volume.

3 Add the uncooked pasta, tomatoes, half-and-half, ½ cup of the Parmigiano-Reggiano cheese, and ¼ teaspoon of salt and toss to combine. Transfer to the prepared baking dish and spread into an even layer. Cover the baking dish with a double layer of aluminum foil, crimping it tightly around the edges to seal. Place the baking dish on the middle oven rack and bake until the pasta is tender and the liquid absorbed, about 50 minutes.

4 Remove the baking dish from the oven and carefully remove the foil. Set the oven to broil on high heat. Divide the ricotta cheese over the pasta in large dollops. Sprinkle the remaining ¼ cup of Parmigiano-Reggiano cheese over the top. Place the baking dish on the top rack and broil until the ricotta starts to brown, 3 to 5 minutes (watch the pasta closely, as broiler intensities vary). Remove from the oven, top with basil, and serve.

The pasta tastes best straight out of the oven, but will keep, covered in the refrigerator, for a few days.

SERVES 4

UMAMI BOMBS:

1½ cups raw cashews

4 tablespoons extra-virgin olive oil

Kosher salt

2 teaspoons sweet paprika

1½ teaspoons garlic powder

½ teaspoon freshly ground black pepper

12 plum tomatoes (about 2½ pounds), halved lengthwise

1 small yellow onion, peeled and finely chopped

2 teaspoons finely chopped fresh thyme or 1 teaspoon dried thyme

1 tablespoon miso paste (I like lighter-colored miso paste here)

1 dried bay leaf

SICK DAY TOMATO SOUP

I make tomato soup whenever I crave an extra helping of comfort. Here I make it with roasted tomatoes, cashew cream (just cashews briefly soaked in water and then blended) for richness, and a little miso for depth and extra umami for my soul. This plus a grilled cheese (like the miso and caramelized onion grilled cheese on page 149), is a stellar combo.

---

1 Place the cashews in a blender jar and cover with 2 cups of room-temperature water. Set aside to soak while you roast the tomatoes.

2 Preheat the oven to 375°F. Line a rimmed sheet pan with parchment paper or a nonstick baking mat.

3 Mix together 3 tablespoons of the oil, 2 teaspoons of salt, and the paprika, garlic powder, and black pepper in a large bowl. Add the tomato halves and toss to combine, coating the tomatoes well with the spice paste.

4 Turn the tomatoes out onto the prepared sheet pan and place them cut side up. Roast until they are very soft and tender, 40 minutes to 1 hour, depending on the ripeness of your tomatoes (less-ripe tomatoes take longer than ripe ones). Remove the tomatoes from the oven and set aside.

5 Heat a medium skillet over medium heat. Place the remaining 1 tablespoon of oil, onion, thyme, and ½ teaspoon of salt in the skillet and cook, stirring occasionally, until the onion is soft, 5 to 6 minutes. If the onion starts to brown, reduce the heat to medium-low.

6 Blend the cashews with their soaking liquid on high speed until completely smooth, 2 to 3 minutes, then pour into a large soup pot. (You don't need to rinse the blender.) Add the tomatoes to the blender jar with the miso paste, sautéed onion, and 2 cups of water and pulse on low speed to chop, then blend on medium until smooth, 1 to 2 minutes.

7 Add the tomato puree to the cashew cream in the pot. Stir together, add the bay leaf, and place over medium heat until warmed through, about 10 minutes, adding more water to make the soup thinner if you like, and more salt to taste. Remove and discard the bay leaf.

8 Divide the soup among four bowls. Serve immediately.

The soup will keep in an airtight container in the refrigerator for up to 5 days, or in a ziplock bag in the freezer for up to 3 months.

CHAPTER

4

EARTHY, MEATY, SMOKY, RICH

Mushrooms are pure plant magic. Not only are they delicious and positively meaty, but they are high in guanylates, one of the three components that make up umami, along with glutamates and inosinates (see page 2). When mushrooms are dried, the umami factor doubles, making them much more savory and powerful—that's why I use dried shiitakes in the Bomb Sauce on page 208. I think of mushrooms as a flavor vehicle: I brown and crisp them, spice and roast them, or use them to infuse a broth like dashi. Because umami becomes stronger when used synergistically, mushrooms are also a great way to boost flavor when used in tandem with other umami ingredients like kombu (as in the aforementioned dashi) or soy sauce.

MAKES ABOUT 7 CUPS

UMAMI BOMBS: ● ●

---

8 ounces fresh
shiitake mushrooms,
trimmed and halved
(or quartered if large)

1-inch piece fresh
ginger, peeled and
sliced ⅛ inch thick

1 large yellow onion,
skin on, quartered

1 cup kombu pieces
(break them into
smaller pieces if
large)

4 dried shiitake
mushrooms (optional)

1½ teaspoons kosher
salt (optional)

1 scallion, trimmed,
white and light green
parts very thinly
sliced on a diagonal

MUSHROOM DASHI

Using umami ingredients together increases their overall effect. Here, the glutamate in the kombu (see box, page 107) exaggerates the savory quality of the guanylate in the mushrooms, making a sea-fortified, light yet flavorful broth that is wonderful on its own or used in just about any recipe that calls for vegetable broth. For extra umami, I add a small handful of dried shiitake mushrooms in addition to the fresh ones. I like to make this dashi to sip on in the wintertime instead of tea. Not only does it keep me warm, but it's excellent to satisfy nearly any kind of hunger pang.

---

1 Combine the fresh mushrooms, ginger, onion, and 9 cups of water in a large pot. Bring to a boil over high heat, reduce the heat to medium, and gently simmer, covered, for 10 minutes.

2 Add the kombu and dried mushrooms (if using), reduce the heat to medium-low, cover, and continue to cook (do not let it boil) for 20 minutes. Turn off the heat, uncover the pot, and let the dashi cool to room temperature.

3 Strain the dashi through a fine-mesh sieve and into a large bowl, using a wooden spoon to press on the solids to extract all of the juices. Taste and add the salt if you like. Serve warm (reheat if necessary), topped with scallions.

The dashi will keep, in an airtight container in the refrigerator, for up to 1 week.

VARIATION

MISO DASHI: Increase the umami factor even more by stirring 1 tablespoon of miso paste per serving into the dashi right after straining. You can warm the miso dashi gently over a low flame, but avoid bringing it to a boil because high heat destroys the miso's nuance and delicacy.

V

SERVES 4

UMAMI BOMBS: ✳ ✳ ✳

½ cup farro

1 teaspoon kosher salt

½ cup quinoa, rinsed and drained

3 tablespoons canola oil

2 portobello mushrooms, stemmed and caps sliced into ¼-inch pieces

1 medium red onion, peeled and finely chopped

2 teaspoons finely chopped fresh rosemary

1 tablespoon maple syrup

3 cups vegetable broth or Mushroom Dashi (page 100), hot

1 cup rolled (old-fashioned) oats

Flaky smoked sea salt, for garnish

SAVORY MUSHROOM BREAKFAST PORRIDGE

I've always been a big fan of a hearty, savory breakfast, and this porridge qualifies in that camp! Here I mix quinoa with oats and farro to create a filling power-grain blend and top it with sautéed mushrooms, fried onions, and just a little maple syrup for a deliciously salty-sweet morning fix. If you're a fan of polenta, you'll love this (and hey, by the way, you can eat it for dinner, too—it's great topped with the sautéed greens on page 56).

1 Place 6 cups of water in a medium saucepan and bring to a boil. Add the farro and ½ teaspoon of salt and cook until the farro starts to soften, about 15 minutes (it won't be cooked through at this point). Add the quinoa, cover the pot so the lid is partially askew, and continue to cook until the farro is tender and the quinoa has uncoiled and is cooked through, about 15 minutes longer. Drain in a fine-mesh sieve (you'll use the pot again in Step 3—there's no need to wash it now).

2 Meanwhile, heat the oil in a large skillet over medium-high heat. Add the mushrooms and the onion and cook, stirring often, until the onion starts to brown, about 5 minutes. Reduce the heat to medium-low, add ½ teaspoon of salt and the rosemary, and continue to cook until the mushrooms are very browned and the onion is caramelized, 20 to 25 minutes longer. Turn off the heat and stir in the maple syrup.

3 While the mushrooms cook, make the oatmeal: In the pot used for the farro and quinoa, bring 2½ cups of the vegetable broth to a simmer over medium-high heat. Add the oats, reduce the heat to low, and cook, stirring, until they soften, 7 to 10 minutes. Stir in the farro and quinoa and add more broth if needed. Continue to cook until everything thickens and comes together a bit, 2 to 5 minutes.

4 Divide the porridge among four bowls, top with the mushroom mixture, and season with flaky smoked salt. Serve immediately.

V

SERVES 4

UMAMI BOMBS: ◉ ◉ ◉

---

6 tablespoons extra-virgin olive oil

2 medium portobello mushrooms, stemmed and caps sliced into ¼-inch cubes

¼ teaspoon kosher salt

2 tablespoons soy sauce

½ teaspoon smoked paprika

5 garlic cloves, peeled and minced

½ teaspoon freshly ground black pepper

½ teaspoon crushed red pepper flakes

2 cups cooked black-eyed peas

6 cups roughly chopped kale, collard greens, or Swiss chard leaves, tough stems removed

MUSHROOM LARDONS
WITH BLACK-EYED PEAS AND GREENS

When you caramelize food, the browning effect can enhance umami by as much as seven or eight times! Here, mushrooms get extra sweet and sticky in the pan, and then they're tossed in some smoked paprika and soy for an extra umami boost. Black-eyed peas and garlicky sautéed greens make this a super-charged, protein- and nutrient-packed plant-based powerhouse. It's extra awesome served with Polenta with Smoked Cheddar and Kale (page 193) or the cornbread on page 42.

1 Heat 3 tablespoons of the oil in a large skillet over medium-high heat. Add the mushrooms and cook, stirring often, until they start to brown, 3 to 4 minutes. Reduce the heat to medium and continue to cook until the mushrooms are very deeply and evenly browned, about 10 minutes longer, reducing the heat to medium-low if they begin to darken too quickly. You want them to shrivel and brown. Add the salt, soy sauce, and smoked paprika and stir until the pan is dry. Transfer the mushrooms to a bowl and set aside.

»

2 Place the remaining 3 tablespoons of oil in the pan with the garlic, black pepper, and crushed red pepper flakes and cook, stirring, until the garlic is fragrant, 30 seconds to 1 minute. Add the black-eyed peas, and once they start sizzling, add the greens. Stir and shift the greens around using a slotted spoon or tongs, and once they start to wilt, after 1½ to 2 minutes, return the mushrooms to the pan. Cook, stirring frequently, until the greens are tender, 2 to 3 minutes more. Turn off the heat and serve.

The mushrooms with black-eyed peas and greens will keep, in an airtight container in the refrigerator, for up to 5 days.

SEA PLANT UMAMI: KOMBU AND DULSE

Also known as kelp, kombu is a thick, flat seaweed known for its umami properties. It is dried and sold in Asian markets and health food stores and is one of the main ingredients of dashi, a Japanese stock made with kombu and dried, fermented, and smoked fish. Buy some kombu and immediately you'll notice a dry, white, chalky substance on the surface—that's the glutamates, natural MSG! All you need to do to introduce them to a dish is to add pieces of kombu to the soup or sauce as it gently simmers (like miso, you never want to hard-boil kombu as it de-intensifies the umami bump).

Many people believe that when the glutamates in kelp combine with an ingredient rich in inosinate (a nucleotide found in fermented fish; see page 2), the umami quality of the dish can intensify by up to eight times! I like adding a strip of kombu to the pot when I'm cooking anything with beans, too, as many believe that glutamates can aid digestion. It's also nice to brew some kombu in water and add a coin of fresh ginger and a squeeze of lemon for a restorative alternative to herbal or black tea in the wintertime.

Dulse is a red lettuce–looking seaweed that a lot of people like to toast and then pulverize and use as a sprinkle on anything from roasted vegetables to pasta. I like to combine it with softened butter for a very savory, almost bacon-like spread. You can also pan-fry large pieces and use it like bacon on a sandwich.

VO

MAKES FOUR 6-INCH PIZZAS
UMAMI BOMBS: ✺ ✺ ✺ ✺

Vegetable oil, for greasing the grill grates

5 tablespoons extra-virgin olive oil, plus extra as needed

1 pound store-bought or homemade pizza dough, divided into 4 equal pieces

1 teaspoon sweet paprika

1 teaspoon garlic powder

½ teaspoon ground cumin

½ teaspoon ground fennel

1½ teaspoons kosher salt

¼ teaspoon freshly ground black pepper

2 medium portobello mushrooms (6 to 8 ounces each), stemmed and caps cut into ½- to ¾-inch cubes

1 medium red bell pepper, halved, seeded, and cut into ½-inch-square pieces

GRILLED PIZZA
WITH SAUSAGE-SPICED MUSHROOMS, PEPPERS, AND ONIONS

I love seasoning portobellos so they take on traditionally meaty flavors, like the "lardons" on page 104, or here in this "sausage" pizza. The oil prevents the dough from sticking when you roll it, so you don't need to use extra flour. I think the oil also makes for a wonderfully seasoned crisp crust. Grilled pizza is similar to stir-fry in that you must have all of your ingredients near the grill and ready to go because everything happens fast (you don't want to risk burning the pizza while you run back to the kitchen to get a forgotten piece of equipment or a plate). To make this vegan, leave off the cheese. I always use metal skewers, but if you're using wooden ones, be sure to soak them in water for 20 minutes before grilling so they don't ignite. No grill? No problem: You can use a grill pan instead.

1 Heat a charcoal or gas grill to medium-high according to the manufacturer's instructions (you can also use a grill pan over high heat). Brush the hot grill grates with a grill brush. Fold a paper towel into quarters and dip it into the vegetable oil, then use long barbecue tongs to grease the grill grates with the oil-saturated towel.

1 medium red onion, peeled, halved, sliced lengthwise ½ inch thick and then crosswise into ½-inch pieces

1 cup Simple Soy Marinara (page 52) or your favorite store-bought marinara

1 pound fresh mozzarella cheese, grated on the large-hole side of a box grater (a heaping 4 cups)

8 large fresh basil leaves, roughly torn

2 Drizzle 1 tablespoon of the olive oil onto a rimmed sheet pan and set the dough on top, leaving space around each ball. Brush 1 tablespoon of olive oil over the tops of the dough balls, then cover with a towel or plastic wrap and set aside while you grill the vegetables.

3 Whisk the remaining 3 tablespoons of olive oil with the paprika, garlic powder, cumin, fennel, salt, and pepper. Add the mushrooms, bell pepper, and onion, tossing them to coat in the spices. Thread the vegetables onto six skewers. Grill the vegetables, turning occasionally, until they are tender and slightly charred on all sides, about 10 minutes. Slide them off the skewers and into a medium bowl.

4 Line a rimmed sheet pan with parchment paper or a nonstick baking mat. Take one round of dough and place it on a cutting board, making sure the underside and topside are both sufficiently coated with olive oil (if they seem dry, pat with a little more olive oil). Use a rolling pin to roll the dough into a roughly 6-inch circle about ⅛ to ¼ inch thick. Set it on the prepared sheet pan. Roll out another piece of dough in the same fashion. (Wait to roll the other pieces of dough.)

>>

5 On another sheet pan or tray, assemble everything you'll need for grilling the pizzas: Set out the bowl with the grilled vegetables, a bowl with the marinara, another with the mozzarella, and another for the basil, plus extra olive oil for drizzling, a grilling spatula, a spoon, and hot mitts. Also bring four dinner plates out to the grill.

6 Move the two rounds of rolled pizza dough to the grill and cook until grill-marked on the bottom, 2 to 3 minutes. Use the spatula to flip the dough over. Spoon ¼ cup of marinara on each round of dough and spread it to about ½ inch from the edge, then sprinkle each pizza with one-quarter of the vegetables and one-quarter of the cheese. Drizzle with a little olive oil, cover, and grill until the cheese melts, 2 to 4 minutes. Use a spatula to transfer each cooked pizza to a plate. Sprinkle each with some of the basil.

7 Roll out the remaining rounds of dough and grill and top them as directed in Step 6. Cut the pizzas into wedges and serve immediately.

**VEG AND
CORNBREAD
BAKE,**
page 112

V

VEG AND CORNBREAD BAKE

FOR THE FILLING

¼ cup canola oil

2 shallots, peeled and finely minced

2 large portobello mushrooms (about 8 ounces each), stemmed and caps chopped into ½-inch pieces (about 6 cups)

1½ teaspoons kosher salt

½ teaspoon freshly ground black pepper

2 large ears of corn, husked and kernels sliced off the cob

2 garlic cloves, peeled and minced

3 pounds ripe tomatoes, cored and roughly chopped

1 can (15 ounces) white beans, rinsed and drained

3 tablespoons soy sauce

½ cup finely chopped fresh basil leaves

This is a beautiful end-of-summer-first-cool-night casserole to bake. It makes the house smell amazing, and is loaded with lovely late-season vegetables like tomatoes and corn. The cornbread topping is a little different than the cornbread on page 42; it has less sugar and is made with coconut oil and coconut milk— and it's vegan. This is an excellent one-pan potluck dish that can be served at room temperature.

1 Adjust an oven rack to the middle position and preheat the oven to 400°F.

2 *Make the filling:* Heat 3 tablespoons of the oil in a large oven-safe skillet over medium-high heat. Add the shallots and cook, stirring, until they start to soften, about 3 minutes. Add the mushrooms, ½ teaspoon salt, and the pepper and cook, stirring often, until they start to soften and brown, 5 to 7 minutes. Stir in the corn and garlic. Once the garlic becomes fragrant, add the tomatoes, beans, and soy sauce, and cook until the tomatoes start to soften, 6 to 10 minutes, stirring often. Stir in the basil.

3 *Make the cornbread topping:* Whisk the flour, cornmeal, sugar, flax meal, baking powder, salt, and pepper together in a large bowl. Whisk the

FOR THE CORNBREAD TOPPING

1 cup all-purpose flour

2/3 cup yellow cornmeal

1/4 cup sugar

2 tablespoons flax meal

1 tablespoon baking powder

1 1/2 teaspoons kosher salt

1/4 teaspoon freshly ground black pepper

1 1/2 cups coconut milk

6 tablespoons coconut oil, liquefied

1 teaspoon distilled white vinegar

1/2 cup thinly sliced scallions, plus extra for garnish

coconut milk, coconut oil, and vinegar together in a medium bowl. Pour the liquid ingredients over the dry ingredients, add the scallions, and use a wooden spoon to stir until well combined.

4 Use a large soup spoon to drop the cornbread mixture over the top of the vegetable filling. Use a butter knife or the back of the spoon to spread the batter out a little (it doesn't need to be perfect, but you want it in a somewhat even layer across the top).

5 Bake until the cornbread is golden brown and the vegetable filling bubbles at the edges, 35 to 40 minutes. Remove from the oven and let cool for 10 minutes. Sprinkle scallions on top, and serve.

The bake is best the day it is made, but will keep, covered in the refrigerator, for 3 days (the topping will absorb the liquid as it sits). Reheat it in the microwave or in a 300°F oven before serving.

SERVES 4

UMAMI BOMBS: ✦ ✦ ✦ ✦

---

3 tablespoons canola oil

2 large Chinese eggplants, stemmed, halved lengthwise, and sliced into 1-inch pieces

1 teaspoon kosher salt

8 ounces shiitake mushrooms, stemmed and caps thinly sliced

1½ cups vegetable broth or Mushroom Dashi (page 100)

3 tablespoons hoisin sauce

2 tablespoons mirin (sweet rice wine)

1 tablespoon soy sauce

4 scallions, trimmed, white and green parts thinly sliced

3 garlic cloves, peeled and minced

1 tablespoon peeled and freshly grated ginger

8 ounces firm tofu, thinly sliced (this is great with smoked tofu, if you can find it)

1 tablespoon cornstarch

2 teaspoons toasted (dark) sesame oil

MUSHROOM AND EGGPLANT STIR-FRY
WITH TOFU AND HOISIN SAUCE

Eggplant is one of my favorite vegetables, especially Chinese eggplant, with its thin pale-purple skin. Chinese eggplant has hardly any seeds and has no bitterness at all, making it a solid eggplant option for anyone who says they don't like eggplant. Sweet from the hoisin sauce, garlicky, and sharp with ginger, this stir-fry is great served with simple steamed white rice, fried rice (page 61), or plain soba noodles. It keeps beautifully and makes a great lunch.

---

1 Heat the canola oil in a large skillet over medium-high heat. Add the eggplant and ½ teaspoon of salt to the skillet and reduce the heat to medium. Cook, stirring often, until the eggplant begins to soften and brown, 5 to 6 minutes. Add the mushrooms and cook until they start to soften, about 2 minutes.

≫

2 Whisk together the vegetable broth, hoisin, mirin, and soy sauce in a medium bowl and set aside.

3 Add half of the scallions, the garlic, and the ginger to the eggplant and cook until fragrant, about 1 minute. Add the vegetable broth mixture and tofu and reduce the heat to medium-low. Cover the skillet and simmer until the eggplant and mushrooms are tender, 3 to 5 minutes.

4 Mix the cornstarch with 1 tablespoon of water in a small bowl. Add it to the skillet and stir, cooking the mixture until you get a few bubbles at the surface, about 1 minute. Stir in the sesame oil and the remaining ½ teaspoon of salt, sprinkle with the remaining scallions, and serve.

The stir-fry will keep, in an airtight container in the refrigerator, for 5 days.

V

SERVES 4; MAKES ¾ CUP OF MISO DRESSING

UMAMI BOMBS: ● ● ●

FOR THE MUSHROOMS

Vegetable oil, for greasing the grill grates

¼ cup extra-virgin olive oil

12 garlic cloves, peeled and minced

1 tablespoon plus 1 teaspoon ground cumin

1 tablespoon plus 1 teaspoon ground coriander

1 tablespoon kosher salt

2 pounds cremini mushrooms, stemmed and halved (quartered if large)

FOR THE DRESSING

2 tablespoons miso paste (preferably white miso)

2 tablespoons tahini paste

3 tablespoons fresh lemon juice, plus extra as needed

½ teaspoon kosher salt, plus extra as needed

¼ cup ice water

1 teaspoon finely chopped fresh flat-leaf parsley

FALAFEL-SPICED GRILLED MUSHROOMS
WITH MISO-TAHINI DRESSING

Falafel-spiced mushrooms on the grill. I mean, c'mon, this is total food perfection! Tossed in a miso-amped tahini sauce, this dish is the very definition of an umami bomb. If using wooden skewers to grill your mushrooms, soak them in water for 20 minutes to prevent them from lighting on fire. You'll use about half of the Miso-Tahini Dressing—the rest keeps in the fridge for up to 1 week. Serve it as a salad dressing, drizzled over roasted vegetables, or atop a grain bowl. The mushrooms "grill" beautifully in a grill pan, too.

---

1 *Prepare the grill:* Heat a charcoal or gas grill to medium according to the manufacturer's instructions (you can also use a grill pan over high heat). Brush the hot grill grates with a grill brush. Fold a paper towel into quarters and dip it into the vegetable oil, then use long barbecue tongs to grease the grill grates with the oil-saturated towel.

2 *Make the mushrooms:* Whisk together the olive oil, garlic, cumin, coriander, and salt in a small bowl. Add the mushrooms and use your fingers to rub the paste all over each one, then thread them onto ten to twelve skewers (it's fine if the mushrooms touch).

3 Grill the mushrooms, turning them once, until they're browned and grill-marked on both sides and tender (they will shrink up a bit), 8 to 12 minutes total. Remove the mushrooms from the grill and slide them from the skewers and into a large bowl. (If using a grill pan, simply cook the mushrooms in the pan, turning them often, until they are grill-marked and tender, 8 to 10 minutes.)

4 *Meanwhile, make the Miso-Tahini Dressing:* Whisk the miso, tahini, lemon juice, salt, ice water, and parsley together in a medium bowl until smooth and creamy. Taste and adjust the salt or lemon juice if needed.

5 Drizzle about half of the tahini sauce over the mushrooms and toss to coat. Serve immediately, with the extra tahini sauce on the side, if desired.

½ loaf of Italian bread, sliced into ½-inch cubes (4½ to 5 cups)

4 tablespoons (½ stick) unsalted butter, melted, plus 1 tablespoon at room temperature

Kosher salt

8 ounces cremini mushrooms, stemmed and caps quartered

2 shallots, finely chopped

1 large russet potato, peeled and cut into ½-inch cubes

1 tablespoon finely chopped fresh thyme leaves

1 tablespoon finely chopped fresh sage leaves

2 tablespoons extra-virgin olive oil

6 large eggs

2 cups whole milk

½ cup crème fraîche or heavy (whipping) cream

8 ounces Parmigiano-Reggiano cheese, grated on the medium-hole side of a box grater (about 2⅔ cups)

SAVORY MUSHROOM, POTATO, AND PARM BREAD PUDDING

Very decadent, very delicious—this bread pudding is a great holiday brunch-type dish. You can use nearly any kind of aged cheese you have on hand, from Gruyère to Fontina, Gouda to Cheddar. The umami presence of mushrooms and aged cheese means that no one will miss their breakfast bacon or sausage at the table. Plus, who doesn't love a starch-on-starch potato-bread mash-up?

1 Adjust an oven rack to the middle position and preheat the oven to 350°F.

2 Place the bread cubes in a large bowl and toss with 2 tablespoons of the melted butter and ¼ teaspoon of salt. Place a wire cooling rack over a rimmed sheet pan and turn the bread out onto it (reserve the bowl). Toast the bread in the oven until golden brown, 8 to 12 minutes. Remove from the oven and set the rack with the bread aside. Return the sheet pan to the oven and increase the oven temperature to 400°F.

3 Place the mushrooms, shallots, potato, thyme, sage, ¾ teaspoon of salt, the oil, and the remaining 2 tablespoons melted butter in the reserved bowl, and toss to combine. Carefully remove the hot sheet pan from the oven and turn the mushroom mixture out onto it, spreading it in an even layer with a wooden spoon. Return the pan to the oven and roast, stirring midway through, until the mushrooms and potatoes are browned and tender, 25 to 30 minutes. Remove the sheet pan from the oven and reduce the oven temperature to 325°F.

4 Whisk together the eggs, milk, crème fraîche, ¼ teaspoon of salt, and all but ¼ cup of the cheese in a medium bowl. Use the 1 tablespoon of room-temperature butter to grease a 9-inch-square baking dish. Put half of the bread in the baking dish followed by half of the mushroom-potato mixture, then pour half of the egg mixture over the top. Add the remaining bread, the remaining mushroom-potato mixture, and the remaining egg mixture, distributing them evenly. Sprinkle the remaining ¼ cup of cheese over the top.

5 Bake until the bread pudding has puffed and bounces back from light pressure, 50 to 60 minutes. Let cool for a few minutes before serving.

The bread pudding will keep, covered in the refrigerator, for 3 days. Reheat it in a 300°F oven until warmed through.

SERVES 4

UMAMI BOMBS: ● ●

FOR THE GRAVY

1 cup raw cashews

8 ounces cremini mushrooms, stemmed and caps quartered

3 tablespoons canola oil

3 garlic cloves, peeled and minced

2 tablespoons finely chopped fresh rosemary

1 to 1½ teaspoons kosher salt

½ teaspoon freshly ground black pepper

FOR THE BREAD CUBES

4 cups sourdough bread cubes (remove the crusts and cut the bread into 1-inch cubes)

2 garlic cloves, peeled and halved

¼ cup extra-virgin olive oil

¼ teaspoon kosher salt

2 sprigs fresh rosemary

Flaky smoked sea salt

2 tablespoons finely chopped fresh flat-leaf parsley or chives

MUSHROOM GRAVY

OVER GIANT "GBD" BREAD CUBES

Gravy over olive oil–fried sourdough bread cubes. Yes, please. Easier than biscuits or grits, this satisfies my craving for Southern-style sausage gravy in a fast-to-table meat-free way. Oh, "GBD" stands for Golden Brown Delicious, by the way—and these chunky croutons most definitely fit their acronym.

---

1 Adjust an oven rack to the middle position and preheat the oven to 425°F. Set a rimmed sheet pan on the middle rack.

2 *Meanwhile, make the gravy:* Place the cashews in a blender jar, add 2 cups of water, and set aside to soak.

3 Carefully remove the hot sheet pan from the oven and set it on a heatproof surface. Place the mushrooms, canola oil, minced garlic, chopped rosemary, salt, and pepper on the hot sheet pan and toss to combine. Return to the oven and roast, stirring midway through cooking, until browned, 15 to 18 minutes. Transfer half of the mushroom mixture to the blender with the cashews (and their soaking liquid) and blend until the sauce is thick, creamy, and smooth, about 1 minute.

4 *Make the bread cubes:* Line a plate with a paper towel. Place the bread cubes in a large bowl, add the halved garlic cloves, 2 tablespoons of the olive oil, and the salt and toss together, rubbing the giant croutons with the garlic clove halves to coat them with flavor; remove the garlic and add it to a medium skillet. Pour the remaining 2 tablespoons of olive oil into the skillet with the garlic, add the sprigs of rosemary, and heat over medium-high heat until the garlic and rosemary are fragrant, about 2 minutes. Add a bread cube—it should sizzle immediately; if it doesn't, heat the oil for a minute longer. When the oil is hot enough, add all of the bread cubes and fry, turning occasionally, until golden brown on all sides, 4 to 5 minutes. Transfer to the lined plate and sprinkle with the smoked salt.

5 Pour the gravy into a saucepan and warm gently over low heat. Divide the bread cubes among four bowls and cover each with gravy. Top with the reserved mushrooms and serve immediately, sprinkled with parsley.

MUSHROOM SALAD TART

2 cups (about 1½ ounces) dried shiitake mushrooms

4 cups boiling water

8 tablespoons (1 stick) unsalted butter

3 sprigs fresh thyme

1 sprig fresh rosemary

1 dried bay leaf

1 package (1 pound) frozen phyllo dough, thawed in the refrigerator overnight (see box, page 127)

½ cup ricotta cheese

Kosher salt

3 tablespoons extra-virgin olive oil

1 small red onion, peeled, halved, and thinly sliced

4 cups baby greens (spinach, arugula, or a baby greens blend)

½ lemon

1 wedge Parmigiano-Reggiano cheese, for shaving

Freshly ground black pepper

Dried mushrooms have way more umami-boosting guanylate than fresh mushrooms simply because, like aged cheese or roasted tomatoes, the umami becomes concentrated as the mushrooms age and their water evaporates. They need to be soaked first to tenderize and soften, and then they can be sautéed just like fresh 'shrooms. Here, I combine the warm sautéed mushrooms with baby greens and pile them on ricotta-topped, herb-buttered sheets of flaky phyllo dough. The tart is buttery, flaky, crisp, fresh, and bursting with meaty-umami mushroom notes. I love to add loads of Parm ribbons and serve the tart as a gorgeous (and edible) centerpiece.

---

1 Place the dried mushrooms in a heat-safe bowl and cover with the boiling water. Cover the bowl with plastic wrap and set aside to hydrate for 1 hour, then drain the liquid and thinly slice the mushrooms.

2 Adjust an oven rack to the middle position and preheat the oven to 400°F.

3 Place the butter in a small saucepan and melt over medium heat. Add the thyme, rosemary, and bay leaf and infuse the butter, swirling it in the pan occasionally, for 5 minutes. Turn off the heat and set aside.

4 Line a rimmed baking sheet with parchment paper. Unwrap and unroll the phyllo dough, placing a large, clean kitchen towel over it so it doesn't dry out. Remove and discard the herbs from the butter. Place one sheet of phyllo on the prepared baking sheet and brush it all over with the melted herb-infused butter. Lay another sheet of phyllo on top and brush it with the butter. Repeat the layering and buttering ten more times, brushing any remaining butter over the top sheet.

5 Crumble the ricotta over the phyllo and season with salt. Fold the edges of the phyllo over slightly to make a rim (¾ to 1 inch thick), then place the sheet pan in the oven and bake until the phyllo is golden brown, 25 to 30 minutes. Remove from the oven and set aside.

6 Meanwhile, make the topping: Heat 2 tablespoons of olive oil in a large skillet over medium-high heat. Add the onion and cook, stirring often, until soft and just starting to brown, about 5 minutes. Add the mushrooms and ½ teaspoon of salt and cook, stirring occasionally, until the onions are browned and frizzled and the mushrooms are browned as well, 5 to 7 minutes.

7 Scatter the baby greens over the phyllo and drizzle with the remaining 1 tablespoon of oil. Squeeze the lemon half over the greens and season with a pinch or two of salt. Heap the mushroom-onion mixture over the greens and use a vegetable peeler to shave Parm on top. Sprinkle with pepper, slice, and serve.

The tart is best served within a few hours of baking, but can be stored, covered at room temperature, for up to 1 day. Reheat it in a 325°F oven until the phyllo is crisp.

USING PHYLLO DOUGH

Sheets of phyllo dough are very delicate and crumble easily, which is why you need to keep them covered with a clean, dry kitchen towel. Some people recommend dampening the towel first—I don't, because I find that a wet towel makes the phyllo sheets kind of soft and soggy, and they sometimes even stick together, making them more difficult to separate. If a sheet breaks, you can use melted butter to paste the two parts together after transferring it to the sheet pan (this works best if you use broken sheets as the middle layers for a tart or stack of baked phyllo). To save unused phyllo, roll it up gently, wrap it securely in plastic wrap, and place it back in its box. Refrigerate it and use it within a day or two.

CHAPTER

CARAMELIZED ONIONS

SWEET, SAVORY, CARAMELY, SHARP, PUNGENT

When compared with the amount of glutamates in tomatoes or mushrooms, onions can barely measure up . . . until you caramelize them, that is. Onions have very little moisture and lots of natural sugar—add olive oil, a pinch of salt, and some heat and brown, brown, brown them until they're sticky-sweet or even semi-burned at the edges. I mean, there's a reason people can't seem to step away from the bowl of onion dip at a party, right? Paired with the right ingredients, caramelized onions bring an otherworldly savory-sweet sharpness to eggs, dips, toasts, bread, and more.

There are so many ways to serve caramelized onions, and I include many in this chapter. I oven-caramelize them for onion dip, slow-sauté them for toasts and rice, and hard-fry them for a crispy Korean rice flour pancake. You can even caramelize a big pan of onions, pulverize them in a food processor, and keep the spread in the fridge for sandwiches or to stir into pasta. However you approach them, if you like sweet-savory-salty, you're gonna love this chapter.

CARAMELIZED ONION TOAST

WITH BEETS, TOASTED CARAWAY, AND LABNE

3 medium beets, scrubbed and ends trimmed

6 tablespoons plus 3 teaspoons extra-virgin olive oil

Kosher salt

1 teaspoon caraway seeds

2 medium yellow onions, peeled, halved, and very thinly sliced

1 teaspoon finely chopped fresh thyme leaves

4 slices (½ to ¾ inch thick) rustic country-style bread

1 cup plain labne or Greek yogurt (if using Greek yogurt, it's nice to stir in 1 tablespoon of heavy (whipping) cream or half-and-half to make it silky)

¼ teaspoon freshly ground black pepper

I made a version of this toast in my cookbook Toast *but served it with saffron honey, mint, and pistachios—and most notably, no caramelized onions. Deeply browned, earthy onions paired with the creamy tanginess of labne (a thick and silky Lebanese-style yogurt) is a wonderful match, especially with the sweetness of roasted beets and toasty caraway seeds. Shortcut the recipe by buying pre-roasted beets—you can usually find them in the produce area, vacuum-sealed in a plastic pouch. If you aren't into beets, try this with roasted pears.*

---

1 **Roast the beets:** Adjust an oven rack to the middle position and preheat the oven to 375°F. Set each beet on a square of aluminum foil, drizzle each with 1 teaspoon of the oil, and fold the foil to enclose the beet. Set the beets on a rimmed sheet pan and roast until you can pierce them easily with a paring knife, about 1 hour. Remove the beets from the oven and set aside for 20 minutes before opening the foil. Once the beets are cool enough to handle, peel and then chop them into bite-size pieces. Place them in a medium bowl and toss with 1 tablespoon of the oil and ¼ teaspoon of salt.

2 While the beets roast, place the caraway seeds in a large skillet set over medium heat and toast them, shaking the pan often, until they are fragrant and golden brown, about 2 minutes. Transfer the seeds to a cutting board and set aside.

3 Put 3 tablespoons of the oil in the pan and place over medium-high heat. Add the onions and cook, stirring often, until they start to brown around the edges, 3 to 4 minutes. Reduce the heat to medium, add the thyme, and cook, stirring occasionally, until the onions are frizzled and very browned at the edges, 7 to 8 minutes more (if they brown too quickly, reduce the heat to medium-low). Stir in ½ teaspoon of salt. Taste and add more salt if needed, then transfer the onions to a medium bowl.

4 Adjust an oven rack to the upper-middle position and set the bread on an aluminum foil–lined sheet pan. Drizzle the remaining 2 tablespoons of oil over one side of the bread slices and season with a few pinches of salt. Toast the bread until it is golden on both sides, 1 to 2 minutes per side (watch the bread closely, as broiler intensities vary). Remove from the oven and set on a platter.

5 Cover the caraway seeds on the cutting board with a piece of plastic wrap and use the bottom of a skillet to lightly crush the seeds. Place them in a small bowl with the labne and stir in ¼ teaspoon of salt and the pepper. Divide the labne among the slices of bread. Top with the caramelized onions and roasted beets and serve immediately.

V

¼ cup extra-virgin
  olive oil

4 medium yellow
  onions, peeled and
  finely chopped

1 tablespoon finely
  chopped fresh
  rosemary leaves

1½ teaspoons kosher
  salt

2 tablespoons sugar

2 tablespoons dry
  vermouth

1 tablespoon balsamic
  vinegar

ONION AND ROSEMARY JAM

Is this a jam? A spread? A savory marmalade? Does it matter? Spread it on toast and melt cheese on top; tuck it into a panini before pressing; mix it with ricotta; add a dollop to a pesto or ragu. Just make it and love it, okay?

---

1 Heat the oil in a large skillet over medium-high heat for 2 minutes. Add the onions and cook, stirring often, until they become golden and start to soften, 4 to 5 minutes.

2 Reduce the heat to medium, stir in the rosemary, cover, and cook, stirring every 5 to 8 minutes, until the onions are very deeply brown and sticky, 20 to 25 minutes.

3 Uncover, stir in the salt and sugar, and cook, stirring occasionally, until the onions start to stick to the pan, 3 to 5 minutes.

4 Add the vermouth and vinegar, let sizzle, and stir. Turn off the heat and adjust the salt to taste. Let cool for 15 minutes, then pulse in a food processor until the mixture is semi-smooth, two or three 1-second pulses.

The onion jam will keep, in an airtight container in the refrigerator, for up to 1 week.

CHOPPED ICEBERG
WITH CRISPY, SMOKY ONIONS AND BLUE CHEESE DRESSING

FOR THE SALAD

3 tablespoons extra-virgin olive oil

2 large red onions, peeled, halved, and very thinly sliced

½ teaspoon smoked paprika

¾ teaspoon kosher salt

1 head iceberg lettuce, cored and roughly chopped

2 avocados, halved, pitted, peeled, and chopped

1 large ripe tomato, cored and chopped, or 1 pint grape tomatoes, halved

FOR THE DRESSING

½ cup crumbled blue cheese

3 tablespoons sour cream

2 tablespoons buttermilk

1 tablespoon mayonnaise

2 teaspoons fresh lemon juice, plus extra as needed

¼ teaspoon kosher salt, plus extra as needed

Cold, crisp iceberg lettuce leaves have a great, almost juicy crunch that, if you're honest with yourself, satisfies on a deeper level than baby spinach or romaine. Iceberg, bacon, tomatoes, and blue cheese is a classic combo— instead of bacon, I use smoky, paprika-crisped onions and sprinkle them over the salad for a great umami punch. If you can't find perfect avocados, substitute some black olives instead (I like the oil-cured kind).

1 Adjust an oven rack to the middle position and preheat the oven to 400°F.

2 *Make the salad:* Put the oil, onions, smoked paprika, and salt in a medium bowl and toss to combine. Turn the onions out onto a rimmed sheet pan and roast until tender, browned, and crisp, 30 to 40 minutes, stirring midway through cooking.

3 *Make the dressing:* Place the blue cheese, sour cream, buttermilk, mayonnaise, lemon juice, and salt in a medium bowl and stir to combine. Taste and add more salt if needed.

4 Place the lettuce on a platter. Arrange the avocado on one side and the tomatoes on the other. Spoon the dressing over the top and sprinkle the onions over that. Serve immediately.

CARAMELIZED ONION AND SPINACH DIP

3 medium yellow onions, peeled, halved, and thinly sliced (about 5 cups)

¼ cup extra-virgin olive oil

1½ tablespoons finely chopped fresh rosemary or thyme leaves

4 cups baby spinach leaves

¾ teaspoon kosher salt, plus extra as needed

⅔ cup full-fat sour cream

½ cup mayonnaise

2 tablespoons finely chopped fresh chives or dill

Heaping ¼ teaspoon garlic powder

Potato chips, pita chips, or carrot and celery sticks, for serving

I developed this method of caramelizing onions for my cookbook Sheet Pan Suppers Meatless. *Oven heat is much more gentle and generally more even than stovetop heat, meaning the process of caramelizing is relatively hands-off easy. In this version, I add some spinach to the onions during the last few minutes in the oven, then pulse them together in a food processor before stirring in the dairy and seasonings. It's just as addictive as the original, with just a little extra healthiness from the greens to balance out the bag of potato chips you'll serve alongside!*

1 Adjust an oven rack to the middle position and preheat the oven to 300°F.

2 Place the onions on a rimmed sheet pan and drizzle with the oil. Sprinkle with the rosemary, stir to combine, and cover the sheet pan with aluminum foil. Bake until the onions are soft and wilted, 25 minutes. Uncover the pan, stir the onions, and continue to cook until the onions are deeply sticky and dark, 20 minutes.

3 Add the spinach to the pan, stir again, and continue to bake until the spinach is wilted, about 10 minutes longer. Transfer the spinach and onions to the bowl of a food processor fitted with a metal blade. Add ½ teaspoon of salt and pulse until the mixture is roughly chopped. Add the sour cream, mayonnaise, chives, garlic powder, and the remaining ¼ teaspoon of salt and pulse to combine.

4 Use a rubber spatula to scrape the mixture into a serving bowl and taste with a chip. Add more salt to the dip if needed (this will depend on the saltiness of your chips) and serve.

The dip will keep, in an airtight container in the refrigerator, for 2 days.

(V)

1 medium-large head of cauliflower, cored and separated into florets

1 medium red onion, peeled, halved, and thinly sliced

5 tablespoons extra-virgin olive oil

Kosher salt

2 tablespoons fresh lemon juice

1 tablespoon capers (rinsed if salt-packed), roughly chopped

1 tablespoon finely chopped fresh flat-leaf parsley

½ teaspoon freshly ground black pepper

SHEET PAN CAULIFLOWER
WITH CRISPY ONIONS AND CAPER-PARSLEY VINAIGRETTE

Come late fall, when I'm looking to make dinner and warm up the house at the same time, this is one of my favorite vegetable dishes to cook. I heat the sheet pan with the oven, so when I add the cauliflower and onions they sizzle, just like they would in a skillet. I make a caper-parsley vinaigrette to add a little salty punch.

1 Adjust an oven rack to the middle position, place a rimmed sheet pan on it, and preheat the oven to 400°F.

2 Put the cauliflower, onion, 3 tablespoons of the oil, and ¾ teaspoon of salt in a large bowl and toss to coat. Turn out onto the hot sheet pan (reserve the bowl). Roast for 20 minutes, then stir and continue roasting until the cauliflower is tender and browned in spots and the onion is crispy, 15 to 20 minutes longer.

3 Place the lemon juice, capers, parsley, ¼ teaspoon of salt, and pepper in the reserved bowl. Add the remaining 2 tablespoons of oil and whisk to combine. Toss the cauliflower into the vinaigrette, then turn out onto a platter and serve.

The cauliflower will keep, in an airtight container in the refrigerator, for 3 days.

3 small or 2 medium beets, ends trimmed and peeled

2 tablespoons extra-virgin olive oil, plus extra for drizzling

Kosher salt

3 large shallots, peeled, halved, and thinly sliced

1 tablespoon canola or grapeseed oil

2 tablespoons tomato paste

1 tablespoon curry powder

1½ cups basmati rice

½ cup finely chopped fresh cilantro leaves

1 cup full-fat plain yogurt

1 lemon or lime, cut into 4 wedges, for serving

BEET AND CARAMELIZED SHALLOT RAITA

WITH CURRIED RICE

Creamy, cool, savory-sweet, and bright with herbs and citrus, this is a simple dish that feels exotic. Raita is a savory Indian yogurt-based condiment that is meant to cool the palate while eating spicy, hot food. I like it with rice, and love the sweetness of roasted beets intermingling with the slightly bitter bite of the caramelized shallot. I cook the rice pilaf-style—it turns a warm orange from the curry and tomato paste and delivers an Indian vibe without an intense cooking investment.

1 Adjust an oven rack to the middle position and preheat the oven to 375°F.

2 Place each beet on a square of aluminum foil and drizzle a little olive oil over the tops. Sprinkle each beet with a pinch of salt, wrap up the foil, and set on a rimmed sheet pan. Set the shallots on the other side of the sheet pan and toss with the remaining 2 tablespoons of olive oil and ½ teaspoon of salt. Roast for 15 minutes, then stir the shallots.

Continue roasting until the shallots are tender, browned, and crisping around the edges, 10 to 15 minutes more; transfer them to a medium bowl. Continue to roast the beets until you can pierce them easily with a paring knife, 10 to 15 minutes longer. Remove the beets from the oven, carefully open the foil, and let them cool completely.

3 While the beets cool, heat the canola oil in a large skillet over medium heat for 1 minute. Add the tomato paste and stir until it dissolves into the oil, then stir in the curry powder. Add the rice and stir to combine. Cook, stirring often, until the grains of rice become slightly opaque, 1 to 2 minutes. Add 2¾ cups of water and 1 teaspoon of salt. Stir once and let the water come to a boil. Reduce the heat to medium-low and simmer until the water no longer covers the rice and there are holes beginning to tunnel into it, 5 to 8 minutes. Cover and continue to cook until the water is completely absorbed and the rice is tender, 7 to 12 minutes longer. Turn off the heat and set aside for 5 minutes, then fluff with a fork. Stir in ¼ cup cilantro.

4 Stir the yogurt, remaining ¼ cup cilantro, and ¼ teaspoon of salt into the shallots in the bowl. Chop the beets and add them to the yogurt mixture, folding them in once (the raita will turn pinker the more you stir).

5 Divide the rice among four bowls, top with a healthy scoop of the raita, and serve immediately with a lemon wedge alongside.

FRENCH ONION GRATIN

1 baguette, sliced
½ to ¾ inch thick

2 tablespoons unsalted
butter at room
temperature, plus
2 tablespoons melted

2 tablespoons extra-
virgin olive oil

3 medium yellow
onions, peeled,
halved, and thinly
sliced

2 garlic cloves,
peeled and halved
lengthwise, plus 2
cloves, peeled and
finely chopped

1 tablespoon finely
chopped fresh thyme
leaves

Kosher salt

½ teaspoon freshly
ground black pepper

½ cup dry white wine
or dry vermouth

2 tablespoons miso
paste

3 cups vegetable broth

12 ounces Gruyère or
Comté cheese, grated
(about 4 cups)

Finely chopped fresh
flat-leaf parsley,
for garnish

This idea began as a French onion soup craving, and then I realized I didn't have enough vegetable stock to make it, so presto: a gratin! It has all of the best parts of a cheesy crock of French onion soup: the caramelized onions, the toasty-garlicky bread, the browned and oozy molten Gruyère cap on top—but it's baked in gratin form, meaning it's all about the oniony bread–soaked business with the cheese on top. I love this for dinner with some blanched green beans on the side. The bread must *be stale for the gratin to be pitch-perfect—I like to let it sit out overnight, but you can just toast it in a low oven until it is thoroughly dried out—otherwise the bread will just turn to mush.*

1 Place the baguette slices on a wire cooling rack and leave out overnight to thoroughly stale.

2 The next day, melt 2 tablespoons of the butter in a large skillet over medium-high heat. Add the oil and the onions and cook, stirring often, until they begin to soften, about 3 minutes. Reduce the heat to medium-low and continue to cook, stirring occasionally, until they are deeply brown and sticky, about 40 minutes.

3 Adjust an oven rack to the middle position and preheat the oven to 425°F.

4 Stir the chopped garlic, thyme, ½ teaspoon of salt, and the pepper into the onions and increase the heat to high. Once the garlic is fragrant and the onions are sizzling, 1 to 2 minutes, pour in the wine and cook, stirring often, until the onions look jammy, 3 to 5 minutes. Stir in the miso and broth, bring to a gentle simmer, then reduce the heat to medium-low and continue to gently simmer until reduced by about a third, 3 to 5 minutes. Turn off the heat.

5 Brush a 2-quart gratin or casserole dish with some of the melted butter. Rub both sides of the bread slices with the halved garlic cloves and then dab one side of each slice with the remaining melted butter; season with a few pinches of salt. Arrange the slices of bread in the gratin dish upright and slightly overlapping. You'll probably be able to fit about two rows of baguette in the dish, filling the center of the dish with the last few pieces.

6 Spoon the onion mixture over the bread, then sprinkle with the cheese. Place the gratin in the oven and bake until the topping is totally melted and golden brown, 20 to 25 minutes (you can turn the broiler on for the last few minutes to toast the top if you like, but watch closely, as broiler intensities vary). Serve sprinkled with parsley.

The gratin will keep, covered in the refrigerator, for 3 days. Reheat it in a 350°F oven until warmed through.

CARAMELIZED ONION KOREAN PANCAKE

SERVES 2 TO 4
UMAMI BOMBS: ● ● ●

2 tablespoons canola
  or grapeseed oil

2 large yellow onions,
  peeled, halved, and
  thinly sliced

½ teaspoon plus a
  pinch of kosher salt

¼ cup soy sauce

3 tablespoons rice wine

2 teaspoons rice vinegar

1 teaspoon toasted
  (dark) sesame oil

1 scallion, trimmed,
  white and light green
  parts finely chopped

½ cup rice flour

½ cup all-purpose flour

1 cup ice water

1 large egg, lightly
  beaten

Kimchi, for serving
  (optional)

On weekends, I'll often make this pancake instead of traditional buttermilk pancakes—just for something fun and different. (Leftover caramelized onions in the fridge make this very quick and easy to make on a weekday morning.) You can find rice flour in most health food stores and even in the organic aisle of many supermarkets. Sweet rice flour is a little starchier and, yes, sweeter than regular white rice flour. Both work.

1 Heat the canola oil in a 12- or 14-inch nonstick skillet over medium-high heat. Add the onions and ½ teaspoon salt and cook, stirring often, until the onions start to soften and brown, 4 to 5 minutes. Reduce the heat to medium-low and cook, stirring occasionally, until the onions are deeply browned and sticky, 20 to 25 minutes longer. Remove from the heat and set aside.

2 Meanwhile, stir together the soy sauce, rice wine, rice vinegar, and sesame oil in a liquid measuring cup. Divide among small dipping bowls and sprinkle scallions over the top.

3 Whisk together the rice flour, all-purpose flour, and a pinch of salt in a medium bowl. Add the ice water and egg and stir until the mixture is thick and lump-free. Add half of the caramelized onions.

4 Set the skillet with the remaining onions over medium-high heat and bring them up to a sizzle. Pour the batter over the onions, spreading them out evenly with a silicone spatula, and cook until the underside is set and browned, 2 to 4 minutes.

5 Slide a silicone spatula under the pancake and flip it over. Cook the other side until browned, about 2 minutes.

6 Slide the pancake onto a platter and cut it into wedges. Serve immediately, with the dipping sauce and kimchi, if using.

SERVES 2

UMAMI BOMBS: ● ●

---

4 tablespoons (½ stick) unsalted butter, at room temperature

1 tablespoon extra-virgin olive oil

1 large yellow onion, peeled, halved, and thinly sliced

½ teaspoon kosher salt

1 tablespoon rice vinegar

1 heaping tablespoon miso paste (I like white miso, but a darker miso works, too)

1 tablespoon whole-grain mustard

4 slices good-quality sandwich bread

1 cup grated Gruyère cheese (or ½ cup grated Gruyère with ½ cup grated Gouda for extra umami)

Cornichon pickles, for serving (optional)

CARAMELIZED ONION GRILLED CHEESE
WITH MISO BUTTER

Grilled cheese for dinner feels kind of indulgent, like eating pancakes past 5 pm. Am I right? (Yes.) Here I add miso to the butter I use to swipe the interior of the bread slices (avoid getting too excited and adding the miso butter to the outside of the bread—the miso will burn up before the bread gets toasty and golden), and I add caramelized onions, too. This would also be great with Onion and Rosemary Jam (page 135) instead of the onions.

---

1 Melt 1 tablespoon of butter in a large nonstick skillet set over medium-high heat. Add the oil, onion, and salt and cook, stirring often, until the onion is soft and browned in spots, 8 to 10 minutes. Stir in the vinegar and turn off the heat. Transfer the onion to a small bowl and set aside (don't wash the pan).

2 Mix 1 tablespoon of the remaining butter with the miso paste and mustard in a small bowl. Spread one side of each bread slice with the remaining 2 tablespoons of butter. Spread the other side with the miso butter. Place two of the bread slices, plain buttered side down, in the pan. Divide the cheese and onion evenly between them and top with the other bread slices, plain buttered side up.

3 Cook over medium-low heat until the bread is golden brown, 4 to 5 minutes (do not press the sandwich down with a spatula—just let it be). Flip the sandwiches over and cook on the other side until the bread is golden brown and the cheese is melted, 3 to 4 minutes longer. Transfer to plates and serve immediately with pickles. Lots of pickles.

SERVES 6 TO 8

UMAMI BOMBS: ✹

FOR THE FOCACCIA

2 large yellow onions,
peeled, halved, and
thinly sliced

5 tablespoons extra-
virgin olive oil

½ teaspoon kosher salt

1 pound pizza dough
(homemade or
store-bought)

FOR THE SPICE BLEND

½ cup sesame seeds

2 tablespoons poppy
seeds

2 teaspoons caraway
seeds (optional)

2 tablespoons dried
onion flakes

2 teaspoons garlic
powder

1½ teaspoons kosher
salt

"EVERYTHING BAGEL"
CARAMELIZED ONION FOCACCIA

Focaccia is my go-to dinner party bring-along. Let everyone else bring dips and stews and pasta salad— I'll bring the fresh-from-the-oven bread that will go faster than anything else on the table, guaranteed (well, aside from chocolate chip cookies or brownies, but you know, that's like comparing apples to oranges). The "everything bagel" component of this focaccia is a pantry blend of spices and seeds that work together to give the focaccia a fun, breakfasty twist. If, by some stroke of luck, you have leftovers (or are smart enough to squirrel away a piece for later), eat it toasted with cream cheese for breakfast. You're welcome.

---

1 Adjust an oven rack to the middle position and preheat the oven to 300°F.

2 Place the onions on a rimmed sheet pan, drizzle with 2 tablespoons of the oil, and cover the sheet pan with aluminum foil. Bake until the onions are soft and wilted, 25 minutes. Uncover the pan, stir in the salt, and continue to cook until deeply sticky and dark, 20 minutes. Remove from the oven and transfer to a medium bowl. Increase the oven temperature to 400°F.

3 Grease a jelly roll–style 10-by-16-inch rimmed sheet pan with 1 tablespoon of the remaining olive oil (you can use a 9-by-13-inch baking dish instead, the focaccia will just be a little thinner). Place the pizza dough in the pan and press, push, and pull with your fingers so it fills the pan evenly. Cover with a damp kitchen towel and let it rest for 10 minutes.

4 Mix the spice blend: Stir together the sesame seeds, poppy seeds, caraway seeds (if using), onion flakes, garlic powder, and salt in a small bowl and set aside.

5 Drizzle the remaining 2 tablespoons of oil over the dough and use your fingers to press deep dimples in the dough. Scatter the onions over the top and sprinkle with the spice blend.

6 Bake until the focaccia is browned around the edges, 22 to 26 minutes. Remove from the oven and let cool for 15 minutes, then slide a metal spatula under the focaccia and transfer it to a cutting board. Cut it into squares and serve warm or at room temperature.

The focaccia will keep, wrapped in plastic wrap or aluminum foil, at room temperature for up to 2 days. Reheat it in a 325°F oven before serving.

CHAPTER

FERMENTED, TANGY, SALTY, EARTHY-FUNKY

O f all the umami ingredients in this book, I think that miso paste is the most magical. It is soft and creamy and adds this underlying complexity to nearly anything, from sauces to soups, cookies(!) to pasta. Made from a blend of soybeans and rice, barley, rye, or buckwheat and with koji (a rice fungus) added in, miso is traditionally aged in cedar barrels for a few weeks or up to a few years. You can buy it in small or large tubs, and it's relatively inexpensive.

Miso comes in a few varieties. I use white the most often—it's the mildest and most versatile and is made from a rice base. You can also buy yellow miso, which is made from barley and is a bit stronger than white, or red/brown miso, which is the most intense of the lot, is usually made from buckwheat or other grains, and has a stronger, saltier, more concentrated taste.

Miso is high in glutamates because it is a fermented food. It is also a great source of B_{12} and protein—about 2½ grams per serving. The funky paste is a wonderful addition to so many recipes; you really don't need to stop with the ones in this chapter. Just keep in mind that if you're off-roading with miso, add it to your dish at the end of cooking for the most added value. As with olive oil, the delicate flavors in miso don't hold up to high heat.

GRILLED ASPARAGUS
WITH MISO BUTTER

2 teaspoons vegetable oil, plus extra for greasing the grill grates

1½ pounds thick asparagus (not the pencil-thin kind), tough ends snapped off

¾ teaspoon kosher salt

2 tablespoons miso paste

1 tablespoon unsalted butter, at room temperature

¾ teaspoon garlic powder

Flaky salt, for garnish

Miso combined with soft butter makes a flavorful finishing touch for sauces, pasta, roasted vegetables, or even a grilled cheese (see page 149). Here miso butter combines with the smoke of the grill to add a double dose of umami to a relatively quick veggie dish: grilled asparagus.

1 Heat your charcoal or gas grill to medium according to the manufacturer's instructions (you can also use a grill pan over high heat). Brush the hot grill grates with a grill brush. Fold a paper towel into quarters and dip it into the oil, then use long barbecue tongs to grease the grill grates with the oil-saturated towel.

2 Drizzle the asparagus with the 2 teaspoons of oil and sprinkle with the kosher salt. Place the asparagus on the grill perpendicular to the grill grates and cook, turning, until the asparagus is tender and grill-marked on all sides, 6 to 8 minutes (very thick asparagus may take 1 to 2 minutes longer).

3 *While the asparagus grills, make the miso butter:* Stir together the miso paste, butter, and garlic powder in a small bowl.

4 Transfer the cooked asparagus to a platter and dollop the miso butter over the top. Roll the asparagus around in the butter, sprinkle with flaky salt, and serve immediately.

MORE IDEAS FOR MISO BUTTER

Miso butter is so delicious. Make extra (it will keep, wrapped in the refrigerator, for up to 2 weeks) and use it for:

>> Slathering on biscuits with a drizzle of honey

>> Giving richness to mashed potatoes

>> Spreading on toast

>> Finishing couscous or rice

>> Making garlic bread

SERVES 4
UMAMI BOMBS: ✳ ✳ ✳

---

9 to 10 cups bite-size
  vegetable pieces
  (such as broccoli,
  Brussels sprouts,
  asparagus, carrots,
  radishes, cauliflower,
  mushrooms, or
  parsnips)

3 tablespoons canola,
  grapeseed, or olive oil

1 teaspoon kosher salt

2 tablespoons miso
  paste

1 tablespoon soy sauce

1 tablespoon honey
  or agave syrup

2 teaspoons toasted
  (dark) sesame oil

½ teaspoon freshly
  ground black pepper

UMAMI-ROASTED VEGETABLES

*Tossing roasted veggies with a miso glaze is a fast way
to make a workhorse weekday dish extra special. Feel
free to use any vegetables you have lingering in the
fridge, from carrots to cabbage, asparagus to Brussels
sprouts. Quicker-cooking tender veg—say asparagus
or zucchini—should be added after the first 20 minutes
of cooking.*

---

1 Adjust an oven rack to the middle position and
preheat the oven to 425°F.

2 Toss the vegetables with the canola oil and
¾ teaspoon of the salt in a large bowl, and turn
out onto a rimmed sheet pan (save the bowl). Roast,
stirring after 20 minutes, until the vegetables are
browned and tender, 30 to 35 minutes total.

3 Whisk together the miso, soy sauce, honey,
sesame oil, and pepper in the reserved bowl.

4 Remove the vegetables from the oven and toss
in the bowl with the glaze. Sprinkle with the
remaining ¼ teaspoon of salt, then transfer to a
platter and serve.

The roasted vegetables will keep, in an airtight
container in the refrigerator, for 3 days.

V

SERVES 4
(WITH LEFTOVER QUINOA)
UMAMI BOMBS: ✦ ✦ ✦ ✦

FOR THE GRAIN BOWL

1¾ cups quinoa

Kosher salt

Vegetable oil,
  for greasing the
  grill grates

1 large sweet potato
  (preferably a white
  one), scrubbed and
  cut crosswise into
  ½-inch-thick rounds

4 tablespoons extra-
  virgin olive oil

3 tablespoons fresh
  lemon juice

3 scallions, trimmed,
  white and green parts
  finely chopped

2 medium cucumbers,
  seeds removed if
  large, finely chopped

1 large tomato, cored
  and finely chopped

1½ cups finely
  chopped fresh herbs
  (like basil, cilantro,
  mint, or parsley, or a
  combination of herbs)

1 teaspoon ground
  sumac (optional;
  see Note)

½ cup roasted, salted
  sunflower seeds

QUINOA GRAIN BOWL
WITH GRILLED SWEET POTATOES AND MISO-TAHINI DRESSING

I like to make a big batch of quinoa early in the week—I'll use some for grain bowls, add it to my morning oatmeal, and will even make a quinoa stir-fry or quinoa tabbouleh later in the week. My kids love it in their lunch, too—just add some roasted vegetables and a few splashes of soy sauce and they have an incredibly healthy midday meal. Grilled sweet potatoes add a nice smoky element, but you can roast them if you prefer.

---

1 *Make the quinoa:* Place 3 cups of water in a medium saucepan and bring to a boil over high heat. Add the quinoa and 1 tablespoon of salt and return to a boil. Reduce the heat to low, cover the pan, and cook until the water is evaporated and the quinoa is uncoiled and fluffy, 15 to 18 minutes. Turn off the heat. (If the quinoa looks cooked before all of the water is gone, simply drain the quinoa through a fine-mesh sieve and then place it in a large bowl.)

2 While the quinoa cooks, heat a charcoal or gas grill to medium (or heat a grill pan over medium-high heat). Brush the hot grill grate with a grill brush. Fold a paper towel into quarters and dip it into

FOR THE MISO-TAHINI DRESSING

¼ cup tahini
(sesame paste)

2 tablespoons white
miso paste

2 tablespoons fresh
lemon juice

1 tablespoon plus
1 teaspoon soy sauce

¼ cup almond, soy,
or coconut milk

NOTE: *Sumac powder is a reddish spice made from dried berries that is popular in Middle Eastern cooking. It adds a distinctively tangy taste (it's a common ingredient in za'atar). If it is not available at your local supermarket, you can substitute za'atar or order it from Kalustyans.com.*

the vegetable oil, then use long barbecue tongs to grease the grill grates with the oil-saturated towel.

3 Place the sweet potato rounds in a medium bowl and toss with 1 tablespoon of olive oil and ½ teaspoon of salt. Set the sweet potato rounds on the grill and cook on both sides until the potatoes are tender and grill-marked, 10 to 14 minutes (reduce the heat to medium or move the sweet potatoes to a cooler part of the grill if they are darkening too quickly). Transfer the sweet potatoes to a cutting board, let cool slightly, then cut into quarters.

4 Whisk together the remaining 3 tablespoons of olive oil, the lemon juice, and 1 teaspoon of salt in a small bowl. Pour the mixture over the quinoa and stir to combine. Add the scallions, cucumbers, tomato, herbs, sumac (if using), and grilled sweet potatoes and stir to combine.

5 *Make the Miso-Tahini Dressing:* Combine the tahini, miso paste, lemon juice, soy sauce, and almond milk in a small bowl. Whisk until smooth.

6 Sprinkle the sunflower seeds over the top of the sweet potatoes and serve immediately with the Miso-Tahini Dressing on the side for drizzling over the salad.

SERVES 4
UMAMI BOMBS:

FOR THE CHILE TOFU

2 tablespoons red miso paste

1 tablespoon plus 1½ teaspoons toasted (dark) sesame oil

1 teaspoon garlic powder

12 ounces firm tofu, cut crosswise into ¼-inch-thick planks

1 tablespoon sambal oelek or gochujang

1 tablespoon mirin (sweet rice wine)

1 tablespoon fresh lime juice

½ teaspoon kosher salt

FOR THE LETTUCE WRAPS

10 to 12 large and pliant lettuce leaves (like butterhead lettuce)

20 to 24 large fresh mint leaves

20 to 24 large fresh basil leaves

¼ cup roasted, salted peanuts, finely chopped

Lime wedges, for serving

CHILE TOFU LETTUCE WRAPS
WITH SMOKED SALT

Here, strong red miso marinade adds bold flavor to tofu for tofu-lettuce wraps stuffed with bright, fresh herbs. You can use white miso instead, but the tofu will have a milder flavor. Sambal oelek is a garlic-chile paste that is commonly available in the Asian aisle of most supermarkets; if you can't find it, use gochujang, a Korean red chile paste that is very flavorful but thicker and a little more intense than sambal oelek. The longer you let the tofu marinate, the more thoroughly the marinade will be absorbed, but 20 minutes is enough to get the flavor in.

1 Whisk the miso paste, 1 tablespoon of the oil, the garlic powder, and 1 tablespoon of water together in a small bowl. Place the tofu in a single layer in a baking dish and use a spoon to dollop the paste over all of the tofu pieces. Rub the paste on the top of the tofu, then turn the pieces over and coat the other side. Set aside to marinate for at least 20 minutes or refrigerate overnight.

2 Adjust an oven rack to the top position and heat the broiler to high. Line a rimmed sheet pan with a piece of aluminum foil and place all of the pieces of tofu on the prepared pan. Scrape any remaining sesame-miso paste into a medium bowl and set aside. Broil the tofu, flipping it once, until browned and potentially even slightly charred on both sides, 2 to 4 minutes per side (watch the tofu closely, as broiler intensities vary).

3 While the tofu broils, make the dressing: Add the sambal oelek, mirin, lime juice, and salt to the bowl with the sesame-miso paste and whisk until the mixture is smooth. Remove the tofu from the oven and use a spatula to immediately transfer the tofu to the bowl with the dressing. Gently turn the pieces over in the bowl to evenly coat them.

4 Arrange the lettuce leaves on a platter. Place 2 mint leaves and 2 basil leaves on top of each lettuce leaf. Set a piece of tofu on top of the herbs and sprinkle with peanuts. Serve with lime wedges.

The tofu will keep, in an airtight container in the refrigerator, for up to 3 days. Let it come to room temperature before serving, or reheat it in the microwave or a skillet until warmed through.

MISO BROCCOLI
WITH ORECCHIETTE AND PAN-SEARED LEMONS

1 pound dried orecchiette pasta

1 tablespoon kosher salt, plus extra as needed

1 pound bite-size broccoli florets

1 lemon

¼ cup extra-virgin olive oil

2 teaspoons brown mustard seeds

1 pint grape tomatoes, halved

4 garlic cloves, peeled and very thinly sliced

½ teaspoon crushed red pepper flakes

¼ cup miso paste (I like mellow white miso for this dish)

2 tablespoons unsalted butter

Finely grated Parmigiano-Reggiano cheese, for garnish

Browning lemons in a pan with some oil and salt mellows out their bitterness and sweetens up their sour tang. Combined with the sweet creaminess of miso, the lemons are completely neutralized, so you get a bit of acid and brightness in a softer package. I'm always looking for new ways to serve up broccoli, and this is definitely a great one!

1 Bring a medium saucepan of water to a boil over high heat. Add the orecchiette and 1 tablespoon of salt and boil for 6 minutes. Add the broccoli and cook, according to the pasta package directions, until the orecchiette is al dente, usually 3 to 4 minutes longer. Drain, reserving ¾ cup of the cooking liquid. Dry out the pot.

2 Zest the lemon and set the zest aside. Cut the ends off the lemon, then slice away the white pith to expose the flesh. Cut the lemon in half lengthwise, then thinly slice crosswise into half moons. Set aside.

3 Heat the oil in the pasta pot over medium heat. Add the mustard seeds, and once they start to pop, 1 to 2 minutes, increase the heat to high and add the tomatoes. Cook, stirring, until they sizzle and soften, 1 to 2 minutes, then add the garlic, crushed red pepper flakes, and lemon slices. Cook until the garlic is fragrant and the lemon slices start to liquefy, 30 seconds to 1 minute, then add ½ cup of the pasta water. Push the tomatoes to the edges of the pot to make a space in the center and add the miso paste, whisking until the sauce is creamy (don't let it boil). Stir the tomatoes back into the sauce to reincorporate.

4 Turn off the heat and return the pasta and broccoli to the pot with the butter, stirring to combine (add more pasta water if the pasta seems dry, and more salt to taste). Divide among four bowls and serve immediately, sprinkled with Parmigiano-Reggiano cheese and the reserved lemon zest.

SALTING BASICS

I have lots of kinds of salt in my kitchen. There is no hard-and-fast rule, but generally speaking, I like to use kosher salt for salting water because it is less expensive than sea salt and easy to add by the pinch. I often use fine sea salt because I like the idea of adding extra natural minerals to my food. I have fine table salt in my pantry, too, and I'll sometimes use it for baking instead of using sea salt. Flaky salts like fleur de sel or Maldon crystals are beautiful finishing salts as they add a bit of texture in addition to seasoning. And smoked salt is a must to add a final hint of woodsy campfire to a dish just before serving.

WHY BACON MAKES EVERYTHING BETTER— AND WHAT TO DO WHEN YOU DON'T EAT IT

There was a moment in American cooking when everything seemed to be made with bacon, topped with bacon, or served with bacon on the side. Cured, preserved, and smoked, bacon is also sweet, so it hits on lots of umami receptors from glutamate to inosinate, the nucleotide most often found in meat (the reason why chicken soup tastes so savory and delicious). Bacon is pretreated with all of these umami-enhancing processes—and *then* it gets fried! This caramelization brings out umami-ness and intensifies it even more, making bacon an extra umami-fortifying ingredient.

If you don't eat bacon, there are lots of ways to get close to its flavor—like searing portobellos, as I do here. In addition to the soy sauce, you could add some maple syrup and even a splash of toasted sesame oil for insane bacon-y flavor in a cleaner, more environmentally kind package. Even just adding bacon-y flavors to a dish will give it a smoky-sweet essence. Try these ingredient combos to add that sweet-smoky flavor (throw in a pinch of salt for that bacon-like effect):

SMOKY	+	SWEET
Smoked paprika		Maple syrup
Chipotle chile powder		Honey
Chipotle chiles		Dark brown sugar
Toasted (dark) sesame oil		Miso and rice wine
Smoked soy sauce		Honey or rice wine
Smoked salt		Bourbon!

1 pound dried spaghetti

1 tablespoon plus ½ teaspoon kosher salt

¼ cup extra-virgin olive oil

3 garlic cloves, peeled and finely minced

1 tablespoon freshly ground black pepper

¼ cup white miso paste

3 tablespoons unsalted butter

⅓ cup grated Pecorino Romano cheese

3 tablespoons nutritional yeast

1 tablespoon finely chopped fresh flat-leaf parsley

MISO CACIO E PEPE

If you are a cacio e pepe traditionalist, then skip this recipe. Otherwise, here is a really tasty version! The miso paste and nutritional yeast used here give the pasta an extra savory note. Parsley isn't a classic addition (then again neither is miso or nutritional yeast), but I like a touch of green.

1 Bring a large pot of water to a boil over high heat. Add the spaghetti and 1 tablespoon of salt and cook, following the package instructions, until the spaghetti is just a little shy of al dente (when you bite into a strand, it still tastes like it needs 1 or 2 minutes more to cook). Drain the spaghetti, reserving ¾ cup of the pasta water. Dry out the pot.

2 Heat the oil in the pasta pot over medium heat. Add the garlic and pepper and cook, stirring often, until the garlic is fragrant, about 1 minute. Add the ¾ cup of pasta water, reduce the heat to low, and add the miso paste. Stir until the sauce is creamy (don't let it boil), then add the remaining ½ teaspoon of salt.

3 Add the butter to the pan and, once it's melted, add the pasta and cook, shaking the pan often and stirring the pasta, until it is tender, 1 to 2 minutes. Add the cheese, nutritional yeast, and parsley, stirring to combine. Turn off the heat, divide among four bowls, and serve immediately.

4 tablespoons (½ stick) unsalted butter

½ cup light brown sugar

3 tablespoons miso paste

¼ cup heavy (whipping) cream

1 teaspoon pure vanilla extract

1 pint vanilla ice cream

Sweetened whipped cream (optional; see box)

Chopped smoked almonds or salted, roasted peanuts

MISO BUTTERSCOTCH SUNDAE

If you're a lover of salty caramel, let me introduce you to your newest sweet fix: miso butterscotch. It's salty-sweet and easier to make than caramel. I love it with ice cream, but it's just as good with crepes or served fondue-style with fresh pineapple chunks, strawberries, and pieces of pound cake for dipping.

1 Melt the butter in a medium nonstick skillet over medium-high heat. Add the sugar and stir until combined. Stir in the miso, then add the heavy cream and vanilla and stir until the butterscotch is bubbling and thick. Turn off the heat.

2 Place some ice cream in each bowl. Drizzle with the butterscotch, add a dollop of whipped cream (if using), sprinkle with smoked almonds, and serve immediately.

HOW TO MAKE WHIPPED CREAM

Place 1 cup of cream in a large bowl or in the bowl of a stand mixer fitted with the whisk attachment. Add 3 tablespoons of sugar and ½ teaspoon of vanilla extract and whip on medium-high speed (or by hand or with a hand mixer) until you have medium-stiff peaks (about 2 minutes using a stand mixer or 2 to 3 minutes with a hand mixer). Serve immediately.

1 cup all-purpose flour

½ teaspoon baking soda

¼ teaspoon baking powder

¼ teaspoon fine sea salt

½ cup natural, well-stirred peanut butter (chunky or smooth)

¼ cup white miso paste

¼ cup coconut oil, liquefied

¾ cup unrefined cane sugar

¼ cup light or dark brown sugar

1½ teaspoons pure vanilla extract

MISO PEANUT BUTTER COOKIES

If miso was ever destined to take cookie shape, a peanut butter cookie is its cookie match. Made with coconut oil, natural peanut butter, and flour, these vegan (yes, vegan!) cookies are crispy around the edges and tender at the middle. Be sure to stir your peanut butter well before using—the oil in natural peanut butter has a tendency to separate. I like to use a fork to do the job.

1 Adjust an oven rack to the center position and preheat the oven to 350°F. Line a rimmed sheet pan with parchment paper or a nonstick baking mat.

2 Whisk the flour, baking soda, baking powder, and salt together in a medium bowl.

3 Stir the peanut butter, miso, coconut oil, sugars, and vanilla together in a large bowl until the mixture is well combined. Add the flour mixture to the peanut butter mixture and stir to combine. Divide the dough into 18 balls, each about the size of a ping-pong ball, and place on the prepared sheet pan. Use the back of a fork to gently press a crosshatch pattern into each (you don't want to flatten them too much).

4 Bake until the edges are browned and feel firm (the center will still feel quite soft), 14 to 17 minutes. Remove from the oven and let cool completely before removing from the sheet pan to a wire rack (the cookies will firm up as they cool).

The cookies will keep, in an airtight container at room temperature, for up to 1 week.

DRESS UP YOUR COOKIES

All it takes is a few extra minutes (okay, maybe a half hour) to dress cookies up for company. You can melt chocolate and put it in a ziplock bag, snip off a corner to make a small hole, and then squeeze the bag to stripe the chocolate across the top of the cookies. Or, keep the chocolate in a deep bowl and dunk half of each cookie in, then place it on a piece of parchment or waxed paper to set up. Or, after 10 minutes in the oven, take a teaspoon and lightly press down on the center of the cookie; after the cookies have finished baking and cooled a bit, add a spoonful of your favorite jam—I like strawberry with these.

CHAPTER

7

SMOKE

WOODSY, WARM, SAVORY, SWEET

Smoke. It brings out the primal in us—whether you eat meat or not, I bet a whiff of a wood-burning stove, the smell of a campfire, the first smell of grilled *whatever* sets your stomach growling. Smoke adds wonderful umami to food, too. Finishing a dish with smoked salt is the easiest way to capture the essence of wood and fire without having to build or light one. Smoked paprika, smoked cinnamon, smoked pepper, and even smoked chocolate are simple ways to add a hint of smoke, too. (Smoked paprika and other spices can be used during the cooking or even marinating process.) I use a smoked black tea called lapsang souchong to add a wonderfully intense smoky quality to tofu. Toasted sesame oil and even smoked olive oil (the latter is harder to find and much pricier than the former) are great used as finishing oils. Of course, you can kick it old school by just grilling your food over live fire (charcoal or hardwood) for the most robust charred-smoky essence. A gas grill, electric grill (or grill pan indoors), or even a broiler gets food smoky, too (and if you add a packet of soaked wood chips to your gas grill before cooking, then you get even more smokiness).

GRILLED ROMAINE

WITH CAESAR-ISH VINAIGRETTE

SERVES 4

UMAMI BOMBS: ✴ ✴ ✴

Vegetable oil,
   for greasing the
   grill grates

2 medium garlic cloves,
   peeled and minced

1 medium shallot,
   minced

1 tablespoon nutritional
   yeast

½ teaspoon Dijon
   mustard

Kosher salt

½ teaspoon freshly
   ground black pepper

Juice of 1 lemon

Extra-virgin olive oil

2 heads of romaine
   lettuce hearts,
   halved lengthwise

4 slices (¼ to ½ inch
   thick) good-quality
   bread

1 wedge Parmigiano-
   Reggiano cheese,
   for shaving

1 tablespoon finely
   chopped chives

Parm, nutritional yeast, and smoke from a grill give this salad a hefty dose of deeply satisfying flavor. You might think grilling lettuce will completely wilt it, but no, it doesn't. It beautifully chars the outer leaves while the inner core remains crisp (and even somewhat chilled if you refrigerate the lettuce before grilling). Caesar salad dressing is traditionally made by emulsifying raw egg yolks with olive oil, garlic, and anchovy, but for grilled lettuce, a lighter egg-free vinaigrette is a better match. I don't add the anchovy, but if you want to make this a quadruple umami bomb, use a fork to mash up a bottled anchovy fillet and mix it into the garlic, shallot, and mustard in Step 2.

1 Heat a charcoal or gas grill to high according to the manufacturer's instructions (you can also use a grill pan over high heat). Brush the hot grill grates with a grill brush. Fold a paper towel into quarters and dip it into the vegetable oil, then use long barbecue tongs to grease the grill grates with the oil-saturated towel.

2 Mix together the garlic, shallot, nutritional yeast, mustard, ¾ teaspoon of salt, and pepper. Whisk in the lemon juice and then slowly whisk in 3 tablespoons of olive oil until the dressing is creamy and emulsified.

3 Brush the cut sides of the romaine lettuce halves with 2 tablespoons of the olive oil. Sprinkle with ¼ teaspoon of salt. Drizzle both sides of each bread slice with some olive oil, then season 1 side of each piece with a pinch of salt. Place the bread and lettuce (cut side down) on the grill and cook until the lettuce is charred around the edges and grill-marked on one side (do not turn it), and the bread is toasted and grill-marked on both sides, 3 to 4 minutes.

4 Transfer the bread to a platter and set the lettuce charred side up on top of the bread. Drizzle the vinaigrette over the lettuce and use a vegetable peeler to shave ribbons of the cheese over the top. Sprinkle with chives and serve immediately.

SERVES 4

UMAMI BOMBS:

3 tablespoons extra-
virgin olive oil

2 large shallots or
1 medium red onion,
peeled and finely
chopped

1 red bell pepper,
halved, seeded,
and finely chopped

Kosher salt and freshly
ground black pepper

8 asparagus spears,
ends snapped, spears
finely chopped

2 garlic cloves, peeled
and minced

8 ounces smoked tofu
(see Note), grated on
the large-hole side
of a box grater (about
2 cups)

1 can (15 ounces) black
beans, rinsed and
drained

3 large eggs, lightly
beaten (optional)

¼ cup salsa,
homemade (page 81)
or store-bought

8 tortillas
(6-inch diameter)

Shredded cheese and
guacamole, for
serving (optional)

SMOKED TOFU BREAKFAST TACOS

Smoked tofu is the key component in these breakfast tacos (but if you can't find it, see the Note on page 185). If you have leftover rice, add it for a smoked tofu breakfast bowl, or if you have large tortillas, wrap it all up burrito-style. Any crunchy vegetable can work in place of the asparagus, like chopped green beans, finely chopped cauliflower or broccoli, or shredded cabbage. Leave the eggs out for vegan tacos.

1 Heat the oil in a large nonstick skillet over medium-high heat for 2 minutes. Add the shallots and bell pepper and cook, stirring often, until they are soft and the shallots start to brown, 5 to 6 minutes.

2 Stir in ½ teaspoon of salt and ½ teaspoon of pepper, then add the asparagus and garlic. Once the garlic is fragrant, after about 2 minutes, stir in the tofu and beans and let them warm through, 3 to 4 minutes.

>>

3 Push the vegetables, beans, and tofu to the perimeter of the pan to make a wide hole in the center. Add the eggs to the center with a pinch each of salt and pepper and stir until they start to set, 2 to 3 minutes (if making vegan tacos, skip this step). Then stir everything together and cook for another 1 to 2 minutes to let the eggs cook through. Stir in the salsa and set aside.

4 Warm the tortillas over an open flame, in a dry skillet, or in the microwave. Place two tortillas on each plate and divide the egg mixture between them. Serve immediately, topped with cheese and guacamole, if using.

NOTE: *Sometimes smoked tofu can be hard to find, so if you can't find it, don't stress—just use regular firm or extra-firm tofu (or veggie crumbles) and add a teaspoon of smoked paprika or chipotle chile powder (if you want it a little spicy) to the mix. Or you can follow the recipe on page 188 to smoke your tofu with lapsang souchong tea—it's quite the extra effort for a breakfast taco, but you could marinate a double batch of tofu and use some for tacos and save the rest for fried rice (see page 61), tofu lettuce wraps (see page 165), or to serve alongside roasted veg (see page 160).*

DAD'S SMOKY EGGPLANT DIP

3 large globe eggplants (about 3 to 3½ pounds total)

1 large red bell pepper (or 1 cup drained, jarred pimento chiles)

½ small yellow onion, peeled and grated on the medium-hole side of a box grater

1¼ teaspoons smoked or plain flaky salt, plus extra as needed

Juice of ½ lemon, plus extra as needed

2 tablespoons neutral oil like canola or grapeseed

2 tablespoons finely chopped fresh flat-leaf parsley

Crudités, crackers, pita wedges, and/or slices of crusty bread, for serving

This is not baba ghanouj. It is a wonderfully smoky and umami-loaded dip that my dad taught me how to make by charring eggplants slowly, scooping out the smoked, silky interior, and then mixing it with roasted pepper, lemon juice, and parsely. You can absolutely broil the eggplants instead of grilling them—the flavor won't be quite as smoky, but the dip will still be very delicious. This is one of those items that keeps getting better after it has sat in the fridge for a few days. The boys and I love it for breakfast dabbed on toast.

1 Using a fork or a paring knife, make a few holes in one side of each eggplant (the holes act like steam vents so your eggplants don't burst while they cook). Adjust an oven rack to the upper-middle position and heat the broiler to high (or prepare a charcoal or gas grill to high).

2 Place the eggplants and red pepper (if using pimento, wait until later to add it) on a foil-lined rimmed sheet pan (or directly on the grill grates) and broil (or grill) until the eggplants start to blacken, about 8 minutes (check often, as broiler intensities vary). Using tongs, turn the eggplants and pepper every 5 to 8 minutes until blackened all over, 10 to 12 minutes for the pepper and up to 15 minutes for the eggplant (you want both ends of the eggplant to be fork-tender).

3 Transfer the red pepper to a bowl and cover the bowl with plastic wrap. Slash the bottom of the eggplants with an X about ½-inch deep into the flesh, and place them stem side up in a colander to allow the liquid to drain out. Once the eggplants are cool enough to handle, transfer them to a cutting board. Cut open an eggplant lengthwise and use a spoon to scrape out the flesh. Repeat with the other eggplants, then chop up the flesh very finely and transfer it to a large bowl. Whisk it a few times to smooth it out and break up any large chunks.

4 Peel the charred skin off the pepper and remove the stem and seeds. Finely chop the roasted pepper (or pimento) and add it and the grated onion to the eggplant. Stir in the salt, lemon juice, oil, and parsley. Taste and add more salt or lemon juice if needed. Cover and refrigerate for 30 minutes to let the flavors come together. Serve with the scoops of your choice (the dip gets even better the next day!).

The dip will keep, in an airtight container in the refrigerator, for 5 days.

SERVES 4

UMAMI BOMBS: ● ●

4 garlic cloves, peeled and smashed

1 teaspoon kosher salt

5 tablespoons lapsang souchong loose-leaf tea (or 8 lapsang souchong tea bags)

1 block (12 to 14 ounces) extra-firm tofu, drained and sliced crosswise ¾ inch thick

2 tablespoons soy sauce

2 tablespoons mirin (sweet rice wine)

1 teaspoon freshly grated ginger

1 tablespoon toasted (dark) sesame oil

2 tablespoons canola or grapeseed oil

2 scallions, trimmed, white, light green, and dark green parts thinly sliced on a diagonal

1 tablespoon toasted sesame seeds (optional; see page 49)

TEA-SMOKED TOFU
WITH SOY-SCALLION SAUCE

Lapsang souchong is a wonderfully smoky black tea. I love to drink it, but it also makes an excellent brine for tofu. Seared the next day and served with a toasty, gingery soy sauce, the tofu is ultra satisfying.

1 Bring a medium saucepan with 5 cups of water, the garlic, and the salt to a boil over high heat. Add the tea, turn off the heat, cover, and set aside for 15 minutes. Strain the mixture into a heat-safe container (discard the tea leaves but keep the garlic in the brine). Add the sliced tofu in a single layer, making sure it is completely submerged. Cover and refrigerate for at least 12 hours or overnight.

2 Whisk the soy sauce, mirin, ginger, and sesame oil together in a medium bowl and set aside.

3 Remove the tofu from the brine and set it on a plate lined with paper towels. Blot the top dry with more paper towels.

4 Heat the canola oil in a large skillet over medium-high heat until it shimmers. Add the tofu and brown on both sides, 2 to 3 minutes per side.

5 Set a piece or two of tofu on each plate, sprinkle with scallions and sesame seeds (if using), and serve immediately with the sauce alongside.

MAKES 8 BURGERS
UMAMI BOMBS: ● ●

---

²/₃ cup whole-grain bulgur

2 teaspoons kosher salt

1 medium sweet potato (about 8 ounces), peeled and cut into 1-inch pieces (or 8 ounces sweet potato puree; see Note)

1 large beet, peeled and shredded (using a food processor or a box grater)

¾ cup walnut pieces

½ cup roughly chopped fresh cilantro, tough stems removed before chopping

2 garlic cloves, peeled and roughly chopped

1 can (15 ounces) black beans, rinsed and drained

2 tablespoons nutritional yeast

1 tablespoon whole-grain mustard

1 tablespoon agave syrup

1½ teaspoons smoked paprika

½ teaspoon freshly ground black pepper

GRILLED BLACK BEAN VEGGIE BURGERS

Smoked paprika, the smoke of a grill, and nutritional yeast give these veggie burgers a leg up on your standard mushroom-based variety. My younger son, who is a vegetarian, detests mushrooms and can taste them from a mile away. So I developed a bulgur–sweet potato–beet combo that works beautifully. Most veggie burgers also have an egg in them and these don't, making them a winner for vegans, too.

It's important to freeze the burgers for at least 30 minutes before cooking so they are nice and chilled and hold their shape when they go on the grill. If you're transporting them to a cookout or outdoor location, freeze them completely, then pack them in a cooler with ice packs so they stay cold—they'll defrost slightly in the cooler, which will make them the perfect consistency when you place them on the grill. Any extra uncooked veggie burgers can be placed back in the freezer until they are completely frozen and then wrapped individually in plastic wrap and sealed in an airtight freezer bag for up to 3 months. Be sure to defrost for 30 minutes to 1 hour before grilling.

1 cup dried bread crumbs (preferably Japanese panko)

2 tablespoons vegetable oil, plus extra for greasing the grill grates

8 burger buns

Burger toppings of your choice, such as pickles, mustard, relish, lettuce, tomato, and/or onions

1 Bring 1½ cups of water to a boil in a medium saucepan over high heat. Stir in the bulgur and ½ teaspoon of salt, cover, and reduce the heat to medium-low. Cook the bulgur until it is tender, about 12 minutes. Turn off the heat and set the bulgur aside, covered.

2 Meanwhile, place the sweet potatoes in a microwave-safe vegetable steamer and steam until they are tender, 3 to 5 minutes. (Alternatively, place them in a stovetop steamer over medium-low heat and steam until they are tender—I start checking around 3 minutes.)

3 Place the shredded beets, walnuts, cilantro, and garlic in a food processor and pulse until finely chopped, about twelve 1-second pulses. Add the sweet potatoes, beans, nutritional yeast, mustard, agave syrup, smoked paprika, remaining 1½ teaspoons of salt, and the pepper and pulse until well combined, about eight 1-second pulses.

4 Scrape the mixture into a large bowl. Add the bread crumbs and cooled bulgur and stir until well combined. Divide the mixture into eight equal portions and shape each into a patty 4 inches wide and ¾ inch thick. Place the burgers in the freezer for at least 30 minutes.

>>

5 Heat a gas or charcoal grill to medium-high heat (you can also use a grill pan over high heat). Brush the hot grill grates with a grill brush. Fold a paper towel into quarters and dip it into the oil, then use long barbecue tongs to grease the grill grates with the oil-saturated towel.

6 Brush both sides of each patty with the 2 tablespoons of oil. Set the patties on the grill and cook, without moving, until grill-marked and browned, 4 to 5 minutes. Use a spatula to flip the patties and grill on the other side until grill-marked and browned, 4 to 5 minutes longer. Transfer the burgers to a platter.

7 Open the buns and grill them cut side down just until they are lightly marked, 1 to 2 minutes. Set a bun on each plate and top with a veggie burger and the toppings of your choice. Serve hot.

NOTE: *If you use premade sweet potato puree, skip Step 2 and add the puree to the food processor in Step 3.*

POLENTA
WITH SMOKED CHEDDAR AND KALE

SERVES 4

UMAMI BOMBS: ●●

---

1 cup polenta

3 teaspoons kosher salt

3 tablespoons extra-virgin olive oil

1 large shallot, peeled, halved, and thinly sliced lengthwise

3 medium garlic cloves, peeled and thinly sliced

½ teaspoon crushed red pepper flakes

1 bunch curly kale, stems removed

2 to 4 tablespoons nutritional yeast (more yeast gives it a more Parmesan-like flavor)

4 ounces smoked Cheddar or Gouda cheese, grated on the medium holes of a box grater (about 1 cup)

2 tablespoons unsalted butter

4 large eggs

Freshly ground black pepper

The woodsy sharpness of smoked Cheddar (or smoked Gouda) adds a rustic quality to this creamy bowl of comfort, while nutritional yeast adds a soft funk and some protein, too. I love this as a hearty meal in the wintertime. I like how the fried egg adds to the sauciness of the dish. If you prefer, a poached egg is also beautiful. Garlicky sautéed mushrooms are an excellent umami addition to the greens.

---

1 Bring 5 cups of water to a boil in a large saucepan or medium heavy-bottomed pot over high heat. Add the polenta and 2 teaspoons of salt. Reduce the heat to medium-low and gently cook, stirring every 5 minutes or so, until the polenta is creamy and all of the large bits are tender and not hard, about 45 minutes.

2 Meanwhile, heat the oil in a large skillet over medium-high heat until it shimmers, about 2 minutes. Add the shallot and cook, stirring occasionally, until it starts to brown around the edges. Reduce the heat to low and add the garlic, crushed red pepper flakes, and ¼ teaspoon of salt, stirring until the garlic becomes golden, 2 to 3 minutes.

Add the kale and another ¼ teaspoon of salt and cook, using tongs to turn the leaves occasionally, until the kale is tender and wilted, 2 to 3 minutes. Turn off the heat and slide the kale into a bowl. Reserve the skillet.

3 Once the polenta is done, stir in the nutritional yeast and the grated Cheddar. Divide among four bowls and top each with some of the kale.

4 Melt the butter in the reserved skillet over medium-high heat. Crack the eggs and add them to the pan, cooking until the whites are cooked through but the yolk is still soft, 3 to 4 minutes. Season with the remaining ½ teaspoon of salt and some pepper to taste. Slide an egg onto each bowl of polenta and serve immediately.

16 cups popped popcorn (from ½ cup kernels if making homemade— or use the Better Than Movie Popcorn on page 211)

8 tablespoons (1 stick) unsalted butter

½ cup lightly packed light brown sugar

¼ cup granulated sugar

Flaky smoked sea salt

⅓ cup heavy (whipping) cream

2 tablespoons toasted (dark) sesame oil

1 teaspoon smoked paprika

½ teaspoon ground cumin

½ teaspoon ground cinnamon

¼ teaspoon baking soda

1 tablespoon sesame seeds

SMOKY SESAME CARAMEL CORN

Sweet and savory—always a great snacking combo! Toasted sesame oil, smoked salt, and smoked paprika give a triple smoky edge to this caramel corn. It's addictive, so watch out.

1 Adjust an oven rack to the upper third of the oven and another to the lower third and preheat the oven to 250°F. Line two rimmed sheet pans with parchment paper or nonstick baking mats. Place the popcorn in a large metal bowl.

2 Melt the butter in a medium saucepan over medium heat. Stir in the brown sugar and granulated sugar and increase the heat to medium-high, stirring constantly. Once the mixture starts to bubble and boil, 1 to 2 minutes, add a few pinches of smoked salt and 3 tablespoons of water. Cook, stirring constantly (scraping the bottom and side of the pan often so nothing burns), until smoke comes off the sugar, about 7 minutes.

»

3 Remove from the heat and immediately add the cream, oil, paprika, cumin, cinnamon, baking soda, and sesame seeds (the caramel will foam up—don't worry, that's normal). Pour the caramel mixture over the popcorn while stirring with a silicone spatula. Once the popcorn is evenly coated, divide it between the prepared sheet pans.

4 Sprinkle the popcorn with a few pinches of smoked salt. Bake until the popcorn starts to crisp, 15 minutes. Stir the popcorn and rotate the pans from top to bottom and bottom to top. Continue baking until the popcorn is glossy and very crispy, 20 to 25 minutes longer. Remove from the oven and set aside to cool completely.

The caramel corn will keep, in an airtight container at room temperature, for up to 1 week (though if it's very humid, it will soften after a couple of days).

1¼ cups all-purpose
flour

½ teaspoon kosher salt

½ teaspoon baking
soda

6 tablespoons unsalted
butter, at room
temperature

2 tablespoons cream
cheese, at room
temperature

½ cup granulated sugar

½ cup light brown
sugar

1 large egg

1 teaspoon pure vanilla
extract

Nonstick cooking spray
(optional)

Smoked flaky salt
(like Maldon),
for sprinkling

24 chocolate truffles,
unwrapped

CHOCOLATE TRUFFLE BOMB COOKIES
WITH SMOKED SALT

I always love the naked bits of cookie in a chocolate chip cookie, so I figured, why not leave the chips out and use the "blondie" base as the cookie, bake it in a mini muffin tin for little two-bite treats, and push a chocolate truffle into the middle of each in lieu of the chocolate chips? A little smoky salt over the top and it's chocolate chip cookie-ish but seems altogether more indulgent and satisfying. I use Lindt truffles for a super molten center, but you can use chocolate kisses, mini peanut butter cups, or squares of your favorite chocolate bar, too.

1 Whisk the flour, salt, and baking soda together in a medium bowl.

2 Mix the butter and cream cheese together with a wooden spoon in a large bowl until creamy. Add the sugars and stir until smooth. Stir in the egg and the vanilla. Add the flour mixture and stir until well combined and no dry patches remain.

»

3 Refrigerate the dough while you preheat the oven to 350°F. Line a mini muffin tin with mini muffin liners (optional; if not using liners, lightly coat each muffin cup with nonstick cooking spray).

4 Divide the dough into 24 balls about the size of ping-pong balls, and place each ball in a prepared muffin cup. Sprinkle the tops with smoked salt.

5 Bake until the dough is just starting to set and become golden, about 10 minutes. Remove the pan from the oven and place a truffle ball in the center of each cookie, pressing down slightly. Return the pan to the oven and continue baking until the cookie dough part is baked through, 5 to 8 minutes longer. Remove from the oven, sprinkle with more flaky salt, and let cool completely in the tin before popping them out and serving.

The cookies will keep, in an airtight container at room temperature, for up to 1 week.

SERVES 4
UMAMI BOMBS:

Vegetable oil, for greasing the grill grates

2 tablespoons agave syrup

2 tablespoons coconut oil, liquefied

¼ teaspoon smoked flaky salt, plus extra for sprinkling

1½ teaspoons sugar

4 large bananas, peeled and left whole

¾ cup semisweet chocolate chips or finely chopped chocolate

½ cup almond milk, cashew milk, or cow's milk

2 tablespoons light corn syrup

1 pint your favorite ice cream (vegan or classic)

Toasted coconut, for serving

Chopped roasted almonds or peanuts, for serving

GRILLED BANANA SPLITS

A little agave syrup and coconut oil brushed over bananas encourages them to caramelize and glisten on the grill. Melting the chocolate into almond milk in a heat-safe bowl on the grill just makes sense since the grill is hot anyway—remember to stir it often so it doesn't burn on the bottom (and set it over the coolest part of the grill to melt it nice and slow). You could make this with pineapples or peaches, too!

1 Heat the grill to medium heat. Brush the grill grates clean. Fold a paper towel into quarters and dip it into the vegetable oil, then use long barbecue tongs to grease the grill grates with the oil-saturated towel.

2 Stir the agave syrup, coconut oil, ¼ teaspoon smoked salt, and sugar together in a small bowl until the sugar is dissolved. Place the bananas on a plate and use a silicone brush to coat them with the agave mixture (you won't use all of it—save the rest to add to the chocolate sauce).

3 Put the chocolate chips and almond milk in a grill-safe saucepan or metal bowl and set on the grill. Stir the chocolate often until it is melted, then stir in the corn syrup and remaining agave mixture.

4 While the chocolate is melting, grill the bananas, turning once, until all sides are browned, 2 to 4 minutes. Use a metal spatula to transfer each one to a bowl.

5 Top each of the bananas with a scoop or two of ice cream, and drizzle with chocolate sauce. Serve immediately, sprinkled with toasted coconut, chopped nuts, and a pinch of smoked flaky salt.

DO MORE WITH GRILLED FRUIT

After dinner is off the grill and the embers are still glowing with nice, even heat—this is the time to grill fruit! Pineapple rings, halved plums, peaches, nectarines, mango, pears, figs, and melon—they're all beautiful with a tinge of smoke. Here are a few ideas for using them post-grill session:

>> Save for morning yogurt or oatmeal

>> Chop and spoon over ice cream

>> Muddle with sugar and mint for a smoky cocktail

>> Add to salad

>> Blend into a smoothie

>> Add to jam for a smoky touch

>> Spoon over toast spread with ricotta

>> Serve over a slice of cake or with whipped cream

CHAPTER

8

NUTRITIONAL YEAST

CHEESY, FUNKY, RICH, SALTY

Don't be scared! Nutritional yeast isn't some funky hippie-era supplement that you sprinkle over food while aligning your chakras. Okay, well, it kind of is (but what you do with your chakras is your own business). Nutritional yeast is a dry and flaky version of yeast that is grown on sugar cane or beets and then harvested, heat-dried, and crumbled to create tasty little flakes. They're kind of cheesy, kind of salty, and just all around good. If you've never tried nutritional yeast, please do! I love it sprinkled over popcorn or used as a fantastic replacement for Parm.

And did I mention how nutritious it is? (I mean, that is why it's called *nutritional* yeast.) It has 18 amino acids, including the nine essential amino acids that humans must get from food, making it a complete protein—and an awesome pantry addition for vegetarians, vegans, and anyone leading a vegetable-forward lifestyle. It's also gluten free and a good source of B vitamins, plus, just one tablespoon of nutritional yeast offers three grams of protein and half your folic acid requirement for the day. You can find it in the spice aisle of most supermarkets—it comes in a big shaker-style container—or some health food stores have it in the bulk aisle. It's inexpensive and delicious, so what's holding you back?

BOMB SAUCE

MAKES 1 3/4 CUPS
UMAMI BOMBS:

---

7 dried shiitake
   mushrooms
   (about ¼ cup)

3 garlic cloves, peeled

1 small red bell pepper

Juice of 1 orange
   (about ⅓ cup)

½ cup tomato paste

¼ cup soy sauce

2 tablespoons miso paste

2 tablespoons
   Worcestershire sauce

2 tablespoons
   nutritional yeast

2 tablespoons dark
   brown sugar

1 tablespoon sherry
   vinegar

1 teaspoon Dijon
   mustard

1 teaspoon kosher salt

1 teaspoon garlic
   powder

1 teaspoon smoked
   paprika

1 teaspoon ground
   ginger

¼ teaspoon cayenne
   pepper

1 tablespoon canola or
   grapeseed oil

Instead of ketchup. Better than barbecue sauce. To give a boost to marinara. For dipping french fries or tots. To dress up a fried egg sandwich. As a glaze for tofu or grilled portobello mushrooms. To dunk tortilla chips. To make the BEST tempeh sloppy joes. As you can see, this umami-loaded Bomb Sauce goes with everything. If you're a vegetarian or vegan, be sure to read the label on your Worcestershire sauce to make sure it doesn't contain anchovies.

---

1 Heat 1 cup of water in the microwave in 30-second increments (or in a small saucepan over low heat) until it is very steamy and hot, 1½ to 2 minutes. Add the dried mushrooms, cover with plastic wrap, and set aside for 15 minutes to soak.

2 Adjust an oven rack to the top position and heat the broiler to high.

3 Place the garlic cloves and the bell pepper on a rimmed sheet pan and broil, turning every few minutes, until the garlic is browned and the pepper is charred on all sides, 4 to 6 minutes for the garlic and 12 to 14 minutes for the bell pepper (watch the garlic and pepper closely, as broiler intensities vary). Place the garlic cloves in a blender and the bell pepper in a bowl to cool for 15 minutes. Once it's cool, place the pepper in a fine-mesh sieve set over a bowl (to catch any juices) and peel away the charred skin. Add

>>

the skin to the blender. Open the pepper, remove and discard the seeds, and add the flesh to the blender along with the reserved juices.

4 Remove the mushrooms from the soaking liquid (save the liquid) and add them to the blender along with the orange juice, tomato paste, soy sauce, miso, Worcestershire sauce, nutritional yeast, brown sugar, vinegar, mustard, salt, garlic powder, paprika, ground ginger, and cayenne pepper. Blend until the mixture is the consistency of a thick barbecue sauce.

5 Heat the oil in a medium saucepan over medium heat. Add the sauce and bring to a gentle simmer. Reduce the heat to medium-low and cook, stirring occasionally until the flavors come together, 2 to 5 minutes (if the sauce seems too thick, add a few tablespoons of the reserved mushroom soaking liquid). Turn off the heat and let cool.

The sauce will keep in an airtight container in the refrigerator for up to 1 week, or in a ziplock bag in the freezer indefinitely.

V

MAKES 16 CUPS
UMAMI BOMBS:

---

3 tablespoons coconut
   oil, liquefied

½ cup popcorn kernels

1 teaspoon fine sea salt,
   plus extra as needed

3 tablespoons
   nutritional yeast

BETTER THAN MOVIE POPCORN

Kind of cheesy, kind of salty, and super addictive, the combination of nutritional yeast and coconut oil is a winner. I love how the coconut oil makes the popcorn a little sweet and the nutritional yeast gives it a savory, Parm-like quality. Sometimes I like to add spices, too—like a pinch of cayenne, curry powder, za'atar (a sesame-oregano Middle Eastern blend), or ras el hanout (a Moroccan spice blend). Or I use this popcorn as the base for Smoky Sesame Caramel Corn (page 196).

---

1 Heat a large heavy-bottomed pot (cast-iron or enamelware works great) over medium-high heat for 1 minute. Place the oil and 3 popcorn kernels in the pot. Once the kernels pop, add the remaining kernels and the salt. Cover the pot and cook, shaking the pot often (keep one hand on the lid when you shake so the cover doesn't come off), until you hear that the popcorn has slowed to one or two pops every 5 seconds or so.

2 Remove the lid and immediately toss the popcorn with the nutritional yeast. Season with more salt to taste, and serve immediately.

SERVES 6 TO 8

UMAMI BOMBS: ✦

¾ cup raw cashews

3 tablespoons canola oil

2 large leeks, trimmed, rinsed well, white and light green parts finely chopped

Kosher salt

5 medium garlic cloves, peeled and minced

2 large russet potatoes, peeled and cut into ½-inch cubes

2 cups broccoli florets

½ fennel bulb, cored and roughly chopped

¼ cup nutritional yeast

1 bunch fresh cilantro (about 2 cups leaves)

CREAMY BROCCOLI SOUP
WITH LEEKS AND POTATOES

No one would ever guess there is no cream in this soup—that's the beauty of cashew cream. It's so rich and luscious that it makes a perfect dairy-free alternative to milk and cream. Blanched broccoli gives this soup its hearty taste, while fennel and cilantro add a nice fresh top note. The nutritional yeast adds to the soup's hearty, decadent backbone.

---

1 Put the cashews in a blender and add 1 cup of water to cover. Let them soak for at least 20 minutes or up to overnight (soaking softens the cashews—the longer they soak, the silkier the cashew cream will be).

2 Heat the oil in a large soup pot over medium heat. Add the leeks and ½ teaspoon of salt and cook, stirring often, until the leeks are tender (lower the heat if they start to brown), 6 to 8 minutes. Add the garlic cloves and cook until they're fragrant, 30 seconds to 1 minute. Add the potatoes and 4 cups of water, reduce the heat to medium-low, and simmer until the potatoes are tender, 12 to 15 minutes.

3 Bring a medium saucepan of water to a boil. Add the broccoli, fennel, and 1 teaspoon of salt and boil until the broccoli and fennel are tender, 6 to 9 minutes. Turn off the heat (don't drain).

4 Add the nutritional yeast and 1 teaspoon of salt to the cashews (and their soaking liquid) in the blender and blend until smooth and creamy, 1 to 2 minutes. Use a slotted spoon to transfer the broccoli and fennel (reserve the cooking liquid) to the blender along with all but a few sprigs of cilantro. Add 1½ cups of the cooking liquid and blend again until smooth and creamy. Add more cooking liquid if the mixture is difficult to blend.

5 Pour the broccoli mixture into the pot with the leeks and potatoes and stir to combine. Add more salt and/or water to taste. Chop the remaining cilantro and sprinkle it on top of the soup before serving.

The soup will keep, in an airtight container in the refrigerator, for 3 days.

SERVES 4
UMAMI BOMBS:

1 pound dried fusilli
pasta (or whatever
shape you like)

1 tablespoon plus
¾ teaspoon kosher
salt

¼ cup pine nuts

4 large garlic cloves,
peeled and quartered

2 cups packed kale
leaves, tough stems
removed

1 cup packed fresh basil
leaves

¼ cup nutritional yeast

¾ cup extra-virgin
olive oil

¼ cup dry vermouth
or white wine

Flaky salt and freshly
ground black pepper
(optional)

KALE PESTO PASTA

Here, raw kale, basil, and nutritional yeast get blitzed up to create a creamy cheese-free pesto. Blending kale with other more familiar flavors is a smart way to introduce this wonderfully healthy green to your dinner table. Vermouth is a really nice alternative to white wine because after opening it you can use it as you need to without worrying about it spoiling—it keeps for months!

1 Bring a large pot of water to a boil over high heat. Add the fusilli and 1 tablespoon of kosher salt and stir. Cook according to the package directions until the fusilli is al dente. Drain, reserving ½ cup of the pasta water. Dry out the pot.

2 Combine the pine nuts, garlic, kale, and ¾ teaspoon of kosher salt in the bowl of a food processor and pulse to chop, then process until pasty. Add the basil and nutritional yeast and, with the machine running, drizzle in the oil and continue to process until the pesto is creamy. Taste and adjust the salt, if needed.

3 Return ⅓ cup of the pasta water to the pot, add the vermouth, and bring to a simmer over high heat. Turn off the heat and toss in the pasta. Add the pesto and toss to combine. Add more pasta water if you want it saucier, plus flaky salt and pepper to taste. Serve immediately.

V

SERVES 4 TO 6
UMAMI BOMBS: ● ● ●

FOR THE MASHED POTATOES

2 large russet potatoes, scrubbed

⅔ cup raw cashews

3 tablespoons nutritional yeast

½ teaspoon kosher salt

½ cup warm nondairy milk

¼ cup extra-virgin olive oil

FOR THE CHILI

3 tablespoons extra-virgin olive oil

1 large yellow onion, peeled and finely chopped

1 medium red bell pepper, halved, seeded, and finely chopped

1 medium green bell pepper, halved, seeded, and finely chopped

Kosher salt

½ teaspoon freshly ground black pepper

1 large zucchini, trimmed and finely chopped

5 garlic cloves, peeled and minced

CHILI SHEPHERD'S PIE

This shepherd's pie has a chili-like base made with veggie crumbles and loads of spices (hence the length of the ingredients list—don't be intimidated!). I top it with mashed potatoes made with cashew cream for richness and nutritional yeast for a cheesy tang. Sometimes I use a cornbread topping instead, like the one on page 113. The mashed potato topping is also great served solo as a side dish.

1 *Start the mashed potatoes:* Bring a large saucepan of water to a boil over high heat. Add the potatoes, cover the pan with the lid askew, reduce the heat slightly (so the water doesn't boil over), and boil until you can easily pierce a potato with a knife, 35 to 45 minutes.

2 *Meanwhile, soak the cashews:* Place the cashews in a blender and add ½ cup of water.

3 *Start the chili:* Heat the oil in a large skillet over medium-high heat. Add the onion, red and green bell peppers, ½ teaspoon of salt, and the black pepper, reduce the heat to medium, and cook, stirring often, until the vegetables just start to brown and stick a bit, about 10 minutes. Stir in the zucchini and cook, stirring occasionally, just until it loses its raw look, 3 to 5 minutes, then stir in the garlic and crushed

½ teaspoon crushed
red pepper flakes

2 tablespoons tomato
paste

1 pacakage (10 to 12
ounces) frozen veggie
crumbles (see Note)

1 tablespoon chili
powder

2 teaspoons sweet
paprika

2 teaspoons dried
oregano

1 teaspoon ground
cumin

1 teaspoon ground
coriander

½ teaspoon smoked
paprika

½ cup lager or ale

1 can (14.5 ounces)
crushed tomatoes

1 can (15 ounces)
pinto beans, drained
and rinsed

2 scallions, trimmed,
white and green parts
finely chopped

½ cup finely chopped
fresh cilantro leaves

NOTE: *Veggie crumbles
(aka textured vegetable
protein) can be found in
the frozen foods aisle of
most supermarkets.*

red pepper flakes. Once the garlic is fragrant, stir in
the tomato paste and then add the veggie crumbles.
Cook until the crumbles lose their frozen look, 2 to 4
minutes, then stir in the chili powder, sweet paprika,
oregano, cumin, coriander, and smoked paprika. Cook
for 1 minute, then add the beer, stirring and scraping
up any browned bits at the bottom of the pan. Stir in
the crushed tomatoes, beans, and ½ teaspoon of salt
and simmer gently over medium-low heat to thicken,
10 minutes. Stir in the scallions and cilantro.

4 Drain the potatoes and let cool to the touch,
10 to 15 minutes. Peel them then mash them
using a potato masher or ricer.

5 Add the nutritional yeast and ½ teaspoon of salt
to the blender with the cashews and their soaking
liquid and blend until the mixture is smooth. Pour the
mixture over the potatoes and stir to incorporate,
then add the warm nondairy milk and the olive oil.
Stir to combine, taste, and add more salt, if needed.

6 Adjust an oven rack to the upper-middle position
and heat the broiler to high.

7 Transfer the chili to a 2½-quart casserole dish
and dollop the potatoes on top, using a spatula
to smooth them out in an even layer. Broil until the
potatoes are browned, 6 to 10 minutes (watch them
closely, as broiler intensities vary). Remove from the
oven and scoop into bowls to serve.

The pie will keep, covered in the refrigerator, for 3 days.
Reheat it in a 300°F oven until warmed through.

EGGPLANT "MEATBALLS"

MAKES 20 GOLF BALL–SIZE MEATBALLS

UMAMI BOMBS:

1½ cups fresh breadcrumbs (from 3 to 4 slices of bread)

½ cup plus 2 tablespoons extra-virgin olive oil

Kosher salt

1 large globe eggplant (1¼ to 1½ pounds)

1 large egg (or 3 tablespoons pureed carrot or sweet potato for the vegan option)

⅔ cup cooked lentils

2 medium garlic cloves, peeled and minced

¼ cup roughly chopped fresh basil leaves

¼ cup roughly chopped fresh parsley leaves

⅓ cup nutritional yeast

½ teaspoon freshly ground black pepper

¼ teaspoon crushed red pepper flakes

1 cup canola or grapeseed oil

Back when I was eating more meat, I used to make meatballs all the time, but these days, I like making these eggplant-based ones instead. I use lentils and an egg to make the meatballs stick together. For a vegan option, I've made them with sweet potato or carrot puree (you can buy a jar of baby food in a pinch), instead of using the egg. The texture is a bit delicate; I especially love them when they break up into a marinara sauce (page 52) for a Bolognese effect. To serve the cooked meatballs with marinara, simply add them to warm sauce and let them soak in it for a couple of minutes, (or longer).

1 Adjust an oven rack to the middle position and preheat the oven to 300°F.

2 Place the breadcrumbs in a medium bowl and toss with 2 tablespoons of the olive oil and ¼ teaspoon of salt. Transfer to a rimmed sheet pan and spread in an even layer. Bake until the breadcrumbs are lightly golden and completely dry, 12 to 15 minutes, stirring midway through. Transfer them to a large plate and set aside. Increase the oven temperature to 375°F.

3 Line the sheet pan with aluminum foil and set the eggplant on top. Prick it 3 to 4 times with a

>>

fork, then roast until a paring knife easily slips into the center, 40 to 50 minutes (it should be very tender throughout). Remove the eggplant from the oven and use scissors to cut an X in the bottom. Transfer it, stem side up, to a colander set in the sink and let it drain and cool for 20 minutes.

4 Set the eggplant on a cutting board and slice it open lengthwise, then scoop out the flesh and place it in the bowl of a food processor (if a few charred bits of skin get into the flesh, it's fine. Add the egg, lentils, garlic, basil, parsley, nutritional yeast, ¾ teaspoon of salt, black pepper, and crushed red pepper flakes and process for 12 one-second pulses to combine. Add the toasted breadcrumbs and pulse 2 or 3 times to combine. Scrape the mixture into a medium bowl, cover with plastic wrap flush against the surface, and refrigerate for at least 20 minutes or overnight.

5 Heat the canola oil and the remaining ½ cup of olive oil in a large, deep, heavy-bottomed skillet over medium-high heat for 2 minutes. Shape the eggplant mixture into golf ball–size pieces and roll them until they are nice and round. Drop one into the oil. It should immediately sizzle and be surrounded by small bubbles—if not, let the oil heat up some more. Add a few more balls to the oil, taking care not to overcrowd the pan. Fry the "meatballs" in batches, browning them on all sides, 3 to 5 minutes for each batch. Transfer to a paper towel–lined plate. Serve immediately.

THE ULTIMATE UMAMI COVER SANDWICH!

Isn't it funny that the cover shot for this book wasn't even originally a recipe, but more of a mashup of awesome umami bits and bobs that we had around during the photo shoot? Put them all together and WOW—you get an off-the-charts umami bomb sandwich just bursting with flavors and textures. So I'll tell you what's in the cover shot . . . but I also encourage you to make your own ultimate umami sandwich by taking the leftover bits of this and that and compiling them into an amalgam of pure tastiness.

TO MAKE THE COVER SANDWICH:

To one side of a split pita (or Everything Bagel Focaccia, page 152) add a swipe of Roasted Tomato Mayo (page 85) and to the other side add a swipe of kale pesto (page 215—or store-bought pesto). Stuff the pita with Roasted Tomatoes (page 74) and some Sheet Pan Cauliflower with Crispy Onions and Caper-Parsley Vinaigrette (page 141). Tuck in a few Eggplant "Meatballs" (page 218) and finally drizzle with a few spoonfuls of Bomb Sauce (page 208). That's how we did it. . . . Now, go make your own!

NO QUESO "QUESO"

Cashew cream is the key in so many recipes to richness and a velvety-smooth texture without using butter, cream, or milk. It's so easy to make, too! I made this "queso" for a New Year's Eve party and served it to kids, and you know what? They couldn't get enough. First they dunked tortilla chips in it, then we poured it all over chili nachos for that cheesy movie-theater vibe. So good!

1 cup raw cashews

6 ounces kabocha squash, skin and seeds removed and cut into 1-inch chunks (or ½ cup squash puree; see Note)

¼ cup nutritional yeast flakes

1½ teaspoons kosher salt

¼ cup your favorite store-bought or homemade salsa (page 81)

Tortilla chips and/or crudités, for serving

NOTE: *Kabocha squash is very dense and sweet and gives the queso its orange-y cheesy color. If you use fresh or canned butternut squash puree instead, add another ⅓ cup of cashews in Step 1 to thicken the queso. For an even deeper orange color, add ⅛ teaspowon of ground turmeric.*

1 Place the cashews in a blender and add water to just cover. Set aside at least 20 minutes or up to a few hours to soak (soaking softens the cashews—the longer they soak, the silkier the cashew cream will be).

2 Place the kabocha squash in a microwave steamer or a stovetop steamer basket and steam until fork tender. Set aside to cool for 10 minutes, then add it (or the squash puree) to the blender, along with the nutritional yeast and salt. Puree the sauce until very smooth, about 30 seconds. If it is very thick, add a few more tablespoons of water (don't make it too thin—it will thin out once you add the salsa!).

3 Add the salsa and blend until smooth, or for a chunkier sauce, transfer the "queso" to a bowl and stir in the salsa. Serve with chips and crudités on the side.

The "queso" will keep, in an airtight container in the refrigerator, for up to 3 days.

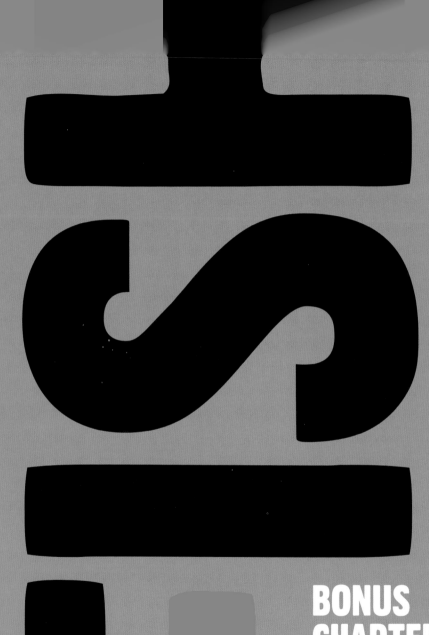

**BONUS
CHAPTER**

UMAMI OF THE SEA

As I mentioned on page 4, I include fish and seafood in my diet about once a week. I always try to choose sustainably raised and in-season seafood. (Did you know that there is actually a season for wild salmon? Late spring through midsummer!) So although this book is about ramping up the umami in vegetable-forward dishes, I wanted to give you some of my favorite fish recipes in case you're inclined to dip a toe into the (literal) waters. Fresh fish and seafood are naturally loaded with umami flavors—in this short chapter, you'll find several recipes that take seafood's inherent savoriness and amplify it with other umami bomb ingredients.

SMOKED TROUT DIP

8 ounces cream cheese, at room temperature

6 tablespoons crème fraîche

½ teaspoon finely grated lemon zest plus 1 tablespoon lemon juice

½ teaspoon kosher salt, plus extra as needed

½ teaspoon freshly ground black pepper

¼ teaspoon garlic powder

8 ounces smoked trout, skin removed

⅓ to ½ cup finely chopped fresh dill (or more if your name is Adeena Sussman)

2 scallions, trimmed, white and light green parts finely chopped

Thick-cut potato chips (preferably ruffled!), for serving

I have a couple of girlfriends who do this cookbook writing thing, too—Sara Kate Gillingham and Adeena Sussman. One night we all congregated around Sara's kitchen island in her Brooklyn home, and we made trout dip while chatting and drinking and cooking (of course). We kept tasting it and adding more and more dill . . . the result is a wonderfully herbaceous smoked trout dip that, strangely, tastes super awesome scooped onto barbecue potato chips!

1 Stir together the cream cheese and crème fraîche in a medium bowl until smooth. Add the lemon zest and juice, salt, pepper, and garlic powder and stir until combined.

2 Flake in the trout and use a fork to blend it in until incorporated (a rough texture is good). Stir in ⅓ cup of dill and the scallions and taste on a chip. Add more dill or salt if needed—how much will depend on the saltiness of your chips.

The dip will keep, in an airtight container in the refrigerator, for 2 days.

FISH SAUCE AND ANCHOVIES

Fresh fish and seafood have lots of natural umami, but ferment or dry them and their umami levels take off. Fermentation is one of the keys to unlocking umami flavor and freeing the amino acids that contribute to it. In fact, one of the most ancient forms of umami is *garum*, a fish sauce that goes back millennia to ancient Greece and Rome. It was made by putting fish in barrels and essentially letting it ferment in the hot sun. The natural enzymes in the fish would break down and liquefy, and there you have it—the original fish sauce. These days, fish sauce is typically made with anchovies and sometimes small dried shrimp (especially in Southeast Asian versions like *nam pla*). Just a dash of fish sauce added to the beginning or end of a dish (add at the end of cooking for a more pronounced "fishy" flavor) will amplify umami.

Anchovies in the tin are also preserved and therefore glutamates are also present in a high quantity. Lots of chefs sneak an anchovy into pasta sauces and salad dressings (puttanesca and Caesar both come to mind) to add an underlying backbone of flavor, salt, and savoriness. Anchovies melted into oil in a hot skillet don't add a "fishy" taste to a dish but more of a robust, salty, *something*. If you're not a vegetarian, definitely try it out.

HONEY-SOY GRILLED SALMON

SERVES 4

UMAMI BOMBS: ● ● ●

¼ cup soy sauce

¼ cup rice wine

2 tablespoons sriracha

2 tablespoons honey

2 tablespoons balsamic vinegar

4 salmon fillets (6 ounces and about ½ inch thick each; preferably wild), skin on, any pin bones removed

Vegetable oil, for greasing the grill grates

1 teaspoon kosher salt

½ teaspoon freshly ground black pepper

1 lime, cut into wedges, for serving

Sweet, spicy, smoky, tangy, umami! This grilled salmon really has it all. I only like to cook wild salmon—I prefer its flavor and the way it is caught. Salmon really is only in season in the late spring and early summer, making this a nice time to get your grilling game on (of course you can buy it frozen, too—and frozen is often fresher than fresh fillets!). If you're using thick farmed salmon, you may need to add a few minutes to the grill time because wild salmon fillets are usually a bit thinner. This glaze works beautifully on grilled tofu, too.

---

1 Whisk together the soy sauce, rice wine, sriracha, and honey in a small saucepan. Bring to a simmer over medium-high heat, reduce the heat to medium-low, and gently simmer until the glaze has reduced by about half and is syrupy, 4 to 6 minutes. Turn off the heat and stir in the balsamic vinegar. Set aside to cool for at least 10 minutes. It will thicken as it sits.

2 Pour three-quarters of the glaze into a 9-inch-square baking dish; set the remainder aside for grilling. Add the salmon fillets, turning them onto each side to coat, then placing them flesh side down into the glaze. Set aside to marinate, at least 15 minutes or up to 1 hour.

3 Heat your charcoal or gas grill to medium-high according to the manufacturer's instructions (you can also use a grill pan over high heat). Brush the hot grill grates with a grill brush. Fold a paper towel into quarters and dip it into the oil, then use long barbecue tongs to grease the grill grates with the oil-saturated towel.

4 Place the salmon on a foil-lined plate or sheet pan and season with the salt and pepper. Transfer the salmon to the grill and cook, flesh side down, covered (if using a charcoal grill, make sure the air vents are open so you don't kill the fire), until the fish is opaque up the sides and has nice grill marks, 3 to 4 minutes (a little longer for thicker fillets).

5 Slide a metal spatula under the fish and flip it over. Grill on the other side until the thickest part of the fish gives only slightly when pressed, about 2 minutes longer. Transfer to a platter and serve immediately with lime wedges alongside.

MISO BROTH AND CLAMS ON TOAST

SERVES 4

UMAMI BOMBS: ● ●

- 8 tablespoons (1 stick) unsalted butter, at room temperature
- 2 scallions, trimmed, white and green parts finely chopped
- 2 tablespoons dry vermouth
- ¼ teaspoon kosher salt, plus extra for sprinkling
- 3 tablespoons white miso paste
- 2 pounds whole raw clams (about 60 cockles or 24 large clams), scrubbed (soak the clams for 20 minutes in cold water if they are very gritty)
- 4 slices (about ¾ inch thick) country-style bread
- 1 tablespoon finely chopped fresh flat-leaf parsley, for garnish
- 1 lemon, quartered, for serving

Vermouth is one of my secret weapons in the kitchen. Unlike white wine, it can be opened and preserved on a shelf in your pantry (or bar cart) for months without losing its herbaceous, sherry-like taste. A little splashed into a pan adds tremendous dimension to a sauce or broth. You could substitute mussels for the clams if you prefer—and be sure to buy the best bread you can find. It makes all the difference! This is killer on the grill, too, and the smoke adds another umami bomb—see the variation on page 232 (if grilling, use only large clams so they don't slip through the grill grates).

1 Melt 6 tablespoons of the butter in a large pot over medium-high heat. Add the scallions, vermouth, and ¼ teaspoon of salt and cook until the scallions are sizzling, 2 to 3 minutes. Stir in the miso.

2 Add the clams to the pot, cover, and cook until they are all opened, 3 to 5 minutes (discard any that don't open).

3 Meanwhile, adjust an oven rack to the upper-middle position and heat the broiler to high.

4 Spread one side of each bread slice with some of the remaining 2 tablespoons of butter and sprinkle with salt. Place the bread buttered side up on a rimmed sheet pan and set on the oven rack. Broil until the bread is toasted, 2 to 4 minutes (watch the bread closely, as broiler intensities vary). Use tongs to turn each bread slice over and toast on the other side, 2 to 3 minutes longer. Place each slice of bread on a plate.

5 Spoon the clams and broth over the bread slices, sprinkle with parsley, and serve immediately, with lemon wedges alongside.

VARIATION

GRILLED TOAST WITH CLAMS AND MISO BROTH: Heat your charcoal or gas grill to medium-high according to the manufacturer's instructions. Brush the hot grill grates with a grill brush. Fold a paper towel into quarters and dip it into vegetable oil, then use long barbecue tongs to grease the grill grates with the oil-saturated towel. Place the 6 tablespoons of butter in a large metal bowl and set on the grill. When the butter has melted, add the scallions, vermouth, and salt and stir to combine. Remove from the heat and stir in the miso. Grill the clams directly on the grates over medium-high heat with the lid closed until the clams open, 3 to 5 minutes. Transfer them to the bowl with the miso broth as they open (discard any that don't open). Grill the buttered bread (beginning buttered side up) instead of broiling it. Serve as described above.

CONVERSION TABLES

Please note that all conversions are approximate but close enough to be useful when converting from one system to another.

OVEN TEMPERATURES

FAHRENHEIT	GAS MARK	CELSIUS
250	½	120
275	1	140
300	2	150
325	3	160
350	4	180
375	5	190
400	6	200
425	7	220
450	8	230
475	9	240
500	10	260

NOTE: *Reduce the temperature by 20°C (68°F) for fan-assisted ovens.*

APPROXIMATE EQUIVALENTS

1 stick butter = 8 tbs = 4 oz = ½ cup = 115 g

1 cup all-purpose presifted flour = 4.7 oz

1 cup granulated sugar = 8 oz = 220 g

1 cup (firmly packed) brown sugar = 6 oz = 220 g to 230 g

1 cup confectioners' sugar = 4½ oz = 115 g

1 cup honey or syrup = 12 oz

1 cup grated cheese = 4 oz

1 cup dried beans = 6 oz

1 large egg = about 2 oz or about 3 tbs

1 egg yolk = about 1 tbs

1 egg white = about 2 tbs

LIQUID CONVERSIONS

U.S.	IMPERIAL	METRIC
2 tbs	1 fl oz	30 ml
3 tbs	1½ fl oz	45 ml
¼ cup	2 fl oz	60 ml
⅓ cup	2½ fl oz	75 ml
⅓ cup + 1 tbs	3 fl oz	90 ml
⅓ cup + 2 tbs	3½ fl oz	100 ml
½ cup	4 fl oz	125 ml
⅔ cup	5 fl oz	150 ml
¾ cup	6 fl oz	175 ml
¾ cup + 2 tbs	7 fl oz	200 ml
1 cup	8 fl oz	250 ml
1 cup + 2 tbs	9 fl oz	275 ml
1¼ cups	10 fl oz	300 ml
1⅓ cups	11 fl oz	325 ml
1½ cups	12 fl oz	350 ml
1⅔ cups	13 fl oz	375 ml
1¾ cups	14 fl oz	400 ml
1¾ cups + 2 tbs	15 fl oz	450 ml
2 cups (1 pint)	16 fl oz	500 ml
2½ cups	20 fl oz (1 pint)	600 ml
3¾ cups	1½ pints	900 ml
4 cups	1¾ pints	1 liter

WEIGHT CONVERSIONS

U.S./U.K.	METRIC	U.S./U.K.	METRIC
½ oz	15 g	7 oz	200 g
1 oz	30 g	8 oz	250 g
1½ oz	45 g	9 oz	275 g
2 oz	60 g	10 oz	300 g
2½ oz	75 g	11 oz	325 g
3 oz	90 g	12 oz	350 g
3½ oz	100 g	13 oz	375 g
4 oz	125 g	14 oz	400 g
5 oz	150 g	15 oz	450 g
6 oz	175 g	1 lb	500 g

ACKNOWLEDGMENTS

Writing a cookbook is no solitary endeavor—there were lots of people who helped make *Umami Bomb* a reality. Thanks to my Grandpa, Charles Sayre, for letting me cash in all of my stocks so I could pay for cooking school and buy myself some knives, pots, and pans (all of which I still have today) back in 1995. I'd like to thank one of my very dearest friends, Stacey Watson, for driving with me from Chicago to Boulder, enduring many truck breakdowns, hot weather, misguided camping adventures, and a blown clutch to get me to Colorado for my first day of cooking school (and thanks to you, Deb and Jen, for more than 30 years of friendship along the way). I'd like to thank Joanne Saltzman, head of The School of Natural Cookery, for teaching me about miso, tamari, dried shiitakes, and nutritional yeast and for introducing me to the big and wonderful world of vegan cooking. And thank you to my cousins Stu and Michelle, for putting up with me and letting me crash at your canyon pad over the summer while I explored my dreams of becoming a chef.

Thank you to my editor, Kylie Foxx McDonald. I love that you love my chocolate cake—thanks for your guidance and great ideas, and for always being open to mine. To the stellar *Umami Bomb* art team, Rae Ann Spitzenberger for design, Kate Sears for photography, Kate Schmidt Buckens for food styling, and Stephanie Hanes for props: Thank you for bringing so much energy and creativity to the art program—your vision really makes the food pop from the page. And to the rest of my Workman family: Anne Kerman, Hillary Leary, Carol White, and Sarah Curley, thank you for helping bring *Umami Bomb* to life. To my agents, Sarah Smith and David Black—thank you for always being supportive, available, and as I've said so many times before, for having my back and leading the way.

To my boys, Julian and Rhys: Thank you for loving vegetables—you guys are so rad, so much fun to cook for, and you make me so proud. Sara and Adeena: You're my sisters, my sounding board, my team. And Marlon, you gently push me in all the right ways; thank you for making every day extra delicious.

RECIPE INDEX

INDEX

ABOUT THE AUTHOR

Award-winning cookbook author Raquel Pelzel has co-authored two dozen cookbooks with creative celebrities like Zac Posen, genius bakers like Uri Scheft, and inspiring chefs like Suvir Saran. She has also written several of her own cookbooks, including *Sheet Pan Suppers Meatless; Toast: The Cookbook;* and *Eggplant*, a Short Stack Editions book. Pelzel was formerly the Food Editor at Tasting Table and an editor for *Cook's Illustrated*. She is a cookbook editor at Clarkson Potter and lives in Brooklyn with her two sons.